✝ransformed

5 Resurrection Dramas

LINDA BONNEY OLIN

Published by Linda Bonney Olin
New York, USA
www.LindaBonneyOlin.com

ISBN: 0991186524
ISBN-13: 978-0991186525

CONTENTS

PREFACE

The premises in these one-act plays are fictional. Obviously Simon Peter and James never appeared on a television talk show! But the featured biblical figures were real people—some of Jesus Christ's closest family and friends. His death and resurrection did, in fact, transform them and their relationships with Jesus. I hope their stories will do the same for you—besides making you laugh and cry a little.

The events mentioned here were drawn from the Bible, with some dramatic license. For example, I paralleled Mary Magdalene's seven demons with the seven deadly sins as a purely fictional device to portray her horrific experience.

"James the Brother of Jesus, Transformed" is presented in two versions. The musical version includes five short songs and broad comedy, as two hecklers dispute James's identity as "brother" of Jesus (Mark 6:3; Galatians 1:19) and question the sincerity of his faith testimony. A shorter version presents James's story as a straightforward interview with glints of humor. This can be presented in settings that do not allow for music, broad comedy, longer running time, or reference to doctrinal disputes.

The *Transformed* dramas began with a Lent dinner/drama series for my local churches. That's a great way to present them, as either Readers Theatre or full productions. I've presented John's monologue and James's interview in lieu of the scripture reading and sermon in worship services, too. Each drama is a standalone piece, but all five together give a sense of the characters' intertwined lives. Although they share the same transformation theme, the variety of drama/comedy, monologue/ensemble, musical/nonmusical, male/female, and modern/biblical elements keeps the series fresh and entertaining.

Running time averages about half an hour for each play (ten to fifteen minutes for the interview version of "James"). Casts are small (one to four speaking parts) and mixed gender. Most roles work well for actors with limited mobility. Staging requirements are minimal.

May you be as richly blessed in reading and performing these plays and songs as I was in writing them! If you enjoy *Transformed: 5 Resurrection Dramas*, please help spread the word to other readers and leave a review on Amazon.com and Christian book discussion web sites. Thanks!

—Linda Bonney Olin

These are written so that you may come to believe that Jesus is the Messiah, the Son of God, and that through believing you may have life in his name.

John 20:31

Scripts

SIMON PETER, TRANSFORMED

Comedy/light drama. The apostle Simon Peter appears on a secular television talk show. He and Andrew, his brother, reveal that Simon Peter was transformed by the resurrection of Jesus Christ from an impulsive, panic-prone follower of Christ to a Christian leader worthy of his nickname, the Rock.

CHARACTERS

INTERVIEWER ~ Hard-nosed TV talk show host. M/F

PETER ~ Simon Peter, an apostle of Jesus; fiftyish or older man.

ANDREW ~ Simon Peter's mischievous younger brother. Likes to rib him in a good-natured way but comes to his defense if an outsider attacks him.

COSTUMES

Contemporary. Business attire for INTERVIEWER and PETER; very casual for ANDREW.

PROPS

Three chairs.

SCENE

The studio of a televised talk show, in the present. The real-life audience serves as the studio audience. There are two empty chairs at center stage. Another empty chair is on the sidelines.

(ANDREW and PETER are sitting in the front row of the audience. INTERVIEWER enters, walks to center stage, and addresses the audience.)

INTERVIEWER: Ladies and gentlemen, we're ready to start taping this evening's broadcast. Please turn off your cell phones and get settled in your seats. Thank you. *(INTERVIEWER preens a bit, then looks straight toward the middle of the audience as if into a camera.)* Here we go. In five, four, three… *(INTERVIEWER pauses two more beats, then speaks in a professional broadcaster's style.)* Welcome to "The Evening Show," your source for no-nonsense analysis of today's news. Our first guest is widely acknowledged as the senior statesman of the Christian church. He found fame as the keeper of the keys of heaven, after declaring his belief that Jesus of Nazareth was the Son of God. He also won critical acclaim for performing miracles, for defying political and religious authorities, and for his compelling oratory. Please help me welcome the apostle Simon Peter.

(PETER walks to center stage as INTERVIEWER leads the audience in applause. They shake hands and sit.)

PETER: Thanks for the applause, but I'm just an ordinary man like the rest of you.

INTERVIEWER *(sardonically)*: You're very modest, for a person who brought dead people back to life.

PETER: Through the power of Jesus Christ, not my own.

INTERVIEWER: Speaking of power, let's talk about your most famous public speech—the powerful sermon of repentance you preached in Jerusalem, on the morning Christians call Pentecost. It was reported that thousands who heard you speak immediately accepted Jesus Christ.

PETER: Yes. You could say the Christian church was born that day.

INTERVIEWER: I found one detail especially fascinating. According to witnesses, the crowd included people from many different countries. Yet each person heard your message in his own language.

PETER: That's right.

INTERVIEWER: Where did you receive your schooling in foreign languages?

PETER: No schooling. I was a fisherman.

INTERVIEWER: So you picked up new languages when your ship docked in foreign ports?

PETER: No, I didn't travel around. My brother Andrew and I operated a small fishing boat on the Sea of Galilee, a good-sized lake in Israel.

INTERVIEWER: Oh. Then how *did* you become fluent in all the languages you spoke on Pentecost?

PETER: Actually, I don't know any foreign languages, except a little Greek.

INTERVIEWER: Then ... ?

PETER *(shrugging)*: It was a miracle. And it wasn't only me, you know. All the apostles preached in strange tongues that day, thanks to the Holy Spirit.

INTERVIEWER: The Holy Spirit? What's that? A translation service?

PETER *(grinning)*: No.

INTERVIEWER: A ghostwriter who composes your speeches for you?

PETER: Well, I do count on the Holy Spirit to give me the right words to say, exactly when I need them. But the Holy Spirit is much more than a communication assistant. The Holy Spirit counsels, encourages, and empowers people who place their faith in Jesus. And confronts those who don't.

INTERVIEWER: Confronts them?

PETER: Sure, to draw the truth out. You talk show people do the same thing, don't you?

INTERVIEWER: Let's keep the spotlight on you, Simon. Er … Peter. Er … Simon Peter … ? Exactly how do you prefer to be addressed?

PETER: You can call me any of those names. My given name is Simon. Jesus nicknamed me Peter, and that's how most people think of me nowadays.

INTERVIEWER: Why Peter?

PETER: Peter means "rock." After I declared my faith in Jesus, the Lord himself said, "You are Peter, and upon this rock I will build my church."

INTERVIEWER: That certainly is a fitting name. Being the oldest apostle, you undoubtedly were a mature, steadying influence on the others.

(ANDREW hoots loudly. He turns and speaks to the audience behind him.)

ANDREW: Simon "mature"? A "steadying influence"? That's a good one!

PETER (to ANDREW): Nobody asked you!

INTERVIEWER (rubbing hands together, smelling a juicy story): Perhaps someone should. (INTERVIEWER turns to Peter with a sly smile.) To draw the truth out. (INTERVIEWER stands and beckons to ANDREW.) Come on up, sir, and tell us who you are. (INTERVIEWER pulls the third chair up next to PETER's chair. ANDREW jogs to center stage, waving to the audience.)

PETER: That "sir" is my brother Andrew. And he's right. You've got the wrong impression of me.

ANDREW: I'll say! I've seen him in action my whole life, and I can tell you—

(PETER gives ANDREW a stern look. ANDREW shakes hands with INTERVIEWER, pats PETER on the shoulder, and sits in a casual slouch in the third chair.)

INTERVIEWER: So, Andrew, you're also an apostle of Jesus of Nazareth?

ANDREW: Hey, I'm the one who put Simon onto Jesus in the first place.

INTERVIEWER: Tell us how that came about.

ANDREW: To begin with, see, I was a disciple of John the Baptist. One day John pointed to Jesus and said, "There's the one I told you about, the man from God." I told my brother, and we went to hear Jesus teach.

PETER: Then Jesus invited us both to be full-time disciples.

ANDREW: Yup. You should've seen it. *(ANDREW holds up his forefingers and thumbs as if framing the scene.)* We're on the lakeshore cleaning our fishing nets. Jesus walks up and says, "Follow me, and I'll make you fishers of men." *(ANDREW gestures with his thumb at PETER.)* So Mr. Stability here *(a beat)* drops his net and runs off with Jesus. Just like that. Left everything right there on the sand—lock, stock, and fishing boat.

INTERVIEWER *(to PETER)*: That seems rather brash. What were you thinking?

PETER: I *wasn't* thinking. Jesus called. I answered. *(PETER looks pointedly at ANDREW.)* You followed the Lord, too, Andrew. So did James and John. *(To INTERVIEWER)* James and John were our partners in that fishing business I told you about. Along with their father, Zebedee.

INTERVIEWER *(to ANDREW)*: Is that true? You followed Jesus on the spur of the moment, too?

ANDREW: Somebody had to tag along and make sure Simon didn't do anything crazy. *(ANDREW turns to the audience.)* A futile effort, as it turned out.

INTERVIEWER *(eagerly prompting ANDREW)*: Peter did something crazy, you say?

ANDREW *(to INTERVIEWER)*: What would you call jumping out of a boat in the middle of the Sea of Galilee?

INTERVIEWER *(to PETER)*: You did that?

PETER: Well, yes. One evening all the apostles were sailing from one lakeside town to another, and suddenly Jesus showed up, walking alongside our boat.

INTERVIEWER: I don't understand. What was Jesus walking on?

PETER: On the water. The Lord called me to join him. So I did.

INTERVIEWER: Let me get this straight. You climbed overboard in the middle of the lake—

ANDREW *(interrupting)*: A very deep lake.

INTERVIEWER: And walked—

ANDREW *(interrupting)*: On the water.

INTERVIEWER: On the water, to Jesus. Who happened to be taking a stroll—

ANDREW *(interrupting)*: Across the lake.

PETER: It seemed like a good idea at the time.

INTERVIEWER: I'd expect that kind of behavior from a reckless kid, not a responsible adult they call the Rock.

ANDREW: Oh, when Simon looked around at the wind and waves and realized he was doing something physically impossible, he behaved exactly like a rock. *(ANDREW makes an exaggerated sinking gesture.)*

PETER *(after a beat, wryly)*: I love you too, brother.

INTERVIEWER: You're sitting here, so obviously you didn't drown.

PETER: No. When I panicked and started to sink, the Lord immediately stretched out his hand to save me. And scolded me for my lack of faith.

INTERVIEWER: Lack of faith? But I'm told there's no disciple more faithful to Jesus than you, Simon Peter.

PETER *(making an exaggerated rocking motion with his hands)*: Yes, but I kept rocking back and forth. One minute I'd see the truth about Jesus so clearly, like a divine revelation, and Jesus would pat me on the back. The next minute, I'd start thinking with my own brain, and spoil everything. Like that time Jesus called me a rock—

INTERVIEWER: That was high praise.

PETER *(making an ascending arm gesture)*: High, all right. I was on top of the world. Until, a few minutes later, Jesus told us he was going to suffer and die in Jerusalem.

ANDREW: The Jewish leaders were out to get him!

PETER: I took Jesus aside and told him no such thing would happen, not if I could help it. Boy, did Jesus give me a look! Said, "Get behind me, Satan!"

INTERVIEWER: That was harsh!

PETER *(making a nosedive hand gesture)*: Brought me down to earth in a hurry, that's for sure. But not too long after that, the Lord took me and James and John up on a mountaintop to pray. *(PETER repeats ascending gesture.)* All of a sudden, Jesus started shining, blazing white. And Moses and Elijah appeared, chatting with him. And then the voice of God spoke, too.

9

INTERVIEWER: Extraordinary!

PETER: I offered to build shelters so Jesus could stay up on the mountain and forget about risking his neck in Jerusalem. *(PETER repeats nosedive gesture.)* Jesus shot down that idea, too.

ANDREW: Then there was the day Jesus fed more than five thousand people with five loaves of bread and two fishes. Remember how Jesus hustled you into the boat afterward?

PETER: Okay, I got carried away with the crowd's plan to make Jesus the King of Israel by force. I thought he'd be pleased.

ANDREW *(to INTERVIEWER)*: He wasn't. *(to PETER)* Don't forget about the foot washing incident. *(to INTERVIEWER)* Simon really put his foot in his mouth that time. Dirt and all.

INTERVIEWER: Foot washing?

ANDREW: When we were in Jerusalem to observe the Passover, Jesus took a bowl of water and knelt in front of us—all the apostles, I mean—to wash our feet.

PETER: I thought, I can't let the Master degrade himself to touch my dirty, stinking feet. I said, "Lord! You're never going to wash my feet!"

ANDREW *(pityingly)*: I saw Jesus give you that "You still don't get it" look.

PETER: Yeah. *(a beat)* Again. Then Jesus warned me, "Unless I wash you, you'll have no part with me."

ANDREW: And my brother, the steadying influence, *(a beat)* did a flip-flop. *(ANDREW turns to the audience and makes a flip-flopping motion with his hands.)* Again.

INTERVIEWER *(to PETER)*: Then you *did* allow Jesus to wash your feet?

PETER: Are you kidding? When he put it like that, I begged him to wash not just my feet, but my hands and my head, too!

INTERVIEWER: A little extreme, don't you think?

ANDREW: That was the Lord's reaction too, as I recall.

INTERVIEWER: Nevertheless, Simon Peter, I don't see how Jesus could fault you for lack of faith in him. Maybe you were rather hasty and misguided at times, but you always worked zealously for Jesus and his ministry.

PETER: That's where you're wrong. My foolish impulses and misguided thinking worked *against* Jesus, not *for* him. That's why he corrected me, again and again, turning me back from the world's way of thinking to God's way. I see that now.

INTERVIEWER: I'm afraid I don't see.

PETER: For example, I was wrong to push Jesus to let the people make him king, because servanthood was what his ministry was all about, not royal privilege. That was the lesson of the foot washing too. But I was too thick-headed to get it.

ANDREW *(tapping the side of his head)*: Solid rock is pretty dense.

PETER: I'm not joking, Andrew. Instead of advising Jesus to steer clear of danger, a true rock would have supported his sacrificial mission. And would have stood by to encourage him through his suffering *(a beat)* all the way to the cross. *(PETER slumps dejectedly.)* In the garden, the night of his arrest, Jesus asked us to watch and pray with him. I couldn't even stay awake.

ANDREW *(encouragingly)*: Don't be so hard on yourself, Simon. The rest of us conked out too, remember? *(He shrugs to the audience.)* It was a *long* day.

11

PETER *(to INTERVIEWER)*: You want to draw out the truth, right? Well, the truth is, I totally failed my dearest friend, my Lord and Savior, that night.

ANDREW *(sitting up and dropping his teasing tone)*: Simon! What are you talking about?

PETER *(to ANDREW)*: Remember, at the Passover meal, I bragged that I would follow Jesus to the death, even if all the others fell away?

ANDREW *(shrugs)*: You were a little cocky. So what?

INTERVIEWER: Witnesses confirmed that you bravely defended Jesus when a contingent of armed men swarmed into the garden to arrest him.

ANDREW *(admiringly)*: Never saw an old fisherman swing a sword the way you did, brother! *(ANDREW turns to the audience.)* Sliced one guy's ear clean off!

PETER *(shaking his head tiredly)*: More misguided zeal. *(PETER turns to INTERVIEWER.)* Jesus told me to put away my sword, and he healed the man I wounded.

ANDREW: Just the same—

PETER: After they bound Jesus and dragged him away, his disciples scattered. The mob took Jesus to the high priest's house. I followed.

ANDREW: There! You were braver than the rest of us, just like you said.

PETER *(bitterly)*: Oh, I stayed at a safe distance, don't worry. Tried to blend in with the people warming themselves at the fire in the courtyard.

INTERVIEWER: Simon Peter, can you put into words for us, what went through your mind while you waited for news of your leader's fate?

PETER: A bunch of misguided ideas, as usual. Mainly, what a disaster this was for Jesus. And how badly it could turn out for all of us disciples. Then, as if she heard my thoughts, one of the servant girls pointed her finger at me and said, "Aren't you a follower of Jesus of Nazareth? You speak like a Galilean, too."

INTERVIEWER: What did you say?

PETER: I said, *(a beat)* "No!" Then someone else asked, "Hey, weren't you with Jesus in the garden?" I said, "No! I don't know the man."

ANDREW *(compassionately)*: Oh, Simon ...

PETER: Then another fellow pushed his way up to me. It was a relative of the man whose ear I cut off.

ANDREW: Uh-oh!

PETER: He said, "I'm sure I saw you in the garden with Jesus! You must be one of his followers!" *(a pause)* I looked at the hostile faces crowding around me and yelled, "No! I don't know what you're talking about!" *(a pause)* As soon as the words left my mouth, a rooster crowed nearby. *(a pause)* And I remembered what Jesus had said at supper, after I vowed I would follow him to the very death. *(PETER wipes his eyes.)* Jesus had told me, "This very night, before the rooster crows, you will disown me three times."

INTERVIEWER: Jesus predicted what you were going to do?

PETER: Yes. He knew me better than I knew myself.

INTERVIEWER: What did you do then?

PETER: Acted on impulse, naturally. *(a beat)* I ran away. And wept.

(PETER hangs his head and covers his face with his hands. ANDREW lays a comforting arm on PETER's shoulder.)

INTERVIEWER *(to the audience, in a hard voice)*: A shocking revelation. Simon Peter, the so-called Rock. In truth: impetuous and irresponsible, inept and uneducated. A coward who publicly disowned the teacher he claimed to love. Are we to believe that Jesus of Nazareth placed such a man in charge of his church? That such a man spoke boldly for Jesus in the face of persecution? *(INTERVIEWER turns to PETER and accuses him harshly.)* What about the Pentecost speech? What about the miracles? Are those reports just a pack of lies?

ANDREW: No!

(PETER raises his head and looks at INTERVIEWER.)

PETER: I did accomplish all those great things for our Lord Jesus Christ. And many more. Because I am not the same Simon Peter who behaved so shamefully.

INTERVIEWER *(taken aback)*: You're an impostor?

ANDREW *(to INTERVIEWER)*: Hold on! I know my own brother when I see him!

PETER *(to INTERVIEWER)*: It's me all right. Simon Peter. The same body, at least. But inside, there's a different me. A better, rock-solid me.

ANDREW *(to INTERVIEWER)*: I'll vouch for that. *(ANDREW turns to audience.)* Did you notice how calmly my brother took it when I teased him? Huh! The old Simon would have hauled off and socked me.

INTERVIEWER *(to PETER)*: You're on tranquilizers?

ANDREW: Get real! Poor fishermen don't have prescription insurance.

INTERVIEWER: What, then? What caused this incredible transformation?

PETER *(solemnly, to INTERVIEWER)*: Nothing but the resurrected Christ.

(INTERVIEWER frowns as PETER turns to the audience.)

PETER: You already know that Jesus was tortured and nailed on a Roman cross to die, while I hid, overcome with fear and sorrow. *(PETER stands and continues with powerful voice and gestures.)* But that wasn't the end of the story, for Jesus or for me. Jesus Christ, the Son of God, arose from his grave, in victory over death!

INTERVIEWER *(scoffing)*: Jesus rising from the dead? That's tabloid talk. No rational human being could believe—

PETER *(interrupting with quiet conviction)*: Of course not. Except through the power of the Holy Spirit.

ANDREW *(with relish)*: Yeah, remember the Holy Spirit?

(INTERVIEWER sighs and rolls eyes.)

PETER: Hey, I can't blame you for being skeptical. When a group of women came back from the empty grave, claiming Jesus was alive, I didn't believe them. But when I saw the risen Lord, heard him speak, and put it all together with the help of the Holy Spirit, I finally *(a beat)* got it. Now, I'm a different man. *(PETER shrugs.)* Judge for yourself, from what I've been able to accomplish by following the spirit instead of my own impulses.

INTERVIEWER: But what about disowning Jesus? You claim Jesus knew that you publicly renounced him.

ANDREW: Sure he knew. He's the Son of God.

INTERVIEWER: I can't believe he would overlook such a betrayal by a trusted disciple.

PETER: No, he didn't overlook it. *(PETER turns to the audience.)* Jesus came and spoke to me after his resurrection.

ANDREW *(nodding vigorously)*: It's true, we all saw him.

PETER: He asked, "Simon, son of Jonah, do you truly love me more than the others?" I said, "Lord, you know how much I love you." He said, "Feed my lambs." Then he asked me again, "Simon, son of Jonah, do you truly love me?" I assured him a second time, "Lord, you know how much I love you." Jesus said to me, "Take care of my sheep." To my surprise, Jesus questioned me a third time, almost as if he were taking an official deposition. "Simon, son of Jonah, do you truly love me?" I answered, "Lord, you know all things, so you know how much I love you." Jesus looked at me and simply said, "Feed my sheep."

INTERVIEWER *(frowning)*: Jesus interrogated you about your love for him—

ANDREW *(interrupting, holding up three fingers to the audience)*: Three times.

INTERVIEWER: Yes, three times, even though—as you said yourself, Simon Peter—if Jesus of Nazareth is the Son of God as you believe, he should know without asking whether you love him or not.

PETER: Yes, he knew. But by formally asking the question, the Lord graciously gave me the chance to formally declare my answer—

ANDREW *(interrupting, holding up three fingers to the audience)*: Three times.

PETER: Yes. I pledged my devotion to Jesus three times, just as I had disowned him ...

(INTERVIEWER and PETER look at ANDREW.)

PETER, ANDREW & INTERVIEWER *(in unison, each holding up three fingers to the audience)*: Three times!

INTERVIEWER: But that business about feeding his sheep? What was that all about?

PETER: Our Lord often compared his followers to a flock of sheep, with himself as their shepherd.

ANDREW: Hey, I get it! *(ANDREW turns to PETER.)* By telling you, over and over, to care for his sheep, Jesus was letting you know he still trusted you to shepherd his believers!

(PETER nods and smiles.)

INTERVIEWER *(grudgingly)*: Okay, I'm beginning to get it, too. In spite of everything, you were forgiven.

PETER: Not just forgiven. Transformed!

(ANDREW stands and applauds, encouraging the audience to join in applause for PETER. INTERVIEWER joins in, reluctantly at first, then stands and applauds heartily.)

INTERVIEWER: Simon Peter, ladies and gentlemen. And his brother, Andrew. *(INTERVIEWER shakes hands with PETER and ANDREW.)* Can you put me in touch with this Holy Spirit?

PETER *(smiling)*: Gladly.

INTERVIEWER *(turning to audience)*: That's our show for this evening. Good night!

(INTERVIEWER, PETER, and ANDREW wave to the audience and exit.)

THE END

MARY MAGDALENE, TRANSFORMED

Monologue, heavier drama, with optional music. Guest speaker/singer Mary Magdalene, from whom Jesus cast out seven demons, describes how Jesus healed, loved, and ultimately transformed her.

CHARACTERS

MAGDALENE ~ Mary Magdalene, devoted disciple and friend of Jesus. Woman in her twenties, thirties, or forties. Speaks passionately, with an undertone of sardonic humor.

COSTUMES

Simple, ankle-length tunic dress. Simple shoes or sandals. No decorative accessories.

PROPS

Full-size wooden cross.

SCENE

Church sanctuary or meeting room, any time. The cross stands downstage right. Otherwise, the stage is bare.

(MAGDALENE stands at center stage looking silently around the audience, making eye contact with as many individuals as possible, for about ten seconds before speaking.)

My name is Mary. A simple, common name. Marys are a denarius a dozen in my part of the world. They call me Mary Magdalene, after my hometown of Magdala. That's a fishing village on the Sea of Galilee.

But there's much more to who a person is, than her name and address, isn't there ...

What I am—that's really what you came to find out. I don't mind. Lots of people are curious about me, and many of them aren't as well-mannered about it as you are.

Believe me, I hear the whispers ... "Mary Maaagdalene ... Isn't she a prosss-titute?" "I heard she's an adulteress!"

The less judgmental types are a bit vaguer in their suspicions, but everyone's sure I'm *some* kind of sinner.

(*MAGDALENE shrugs.*)

I don't deny it. Could you?

You may have heard me described as a woman possessed by seven demons. That much is true. In my culture, the number seven signifies completion, did you know that? Completion. Yes. I was completely possessed ... totally out of my head ... utterly hopeless ...

(*MAGDALENE looks around at the audience and raises her eyebrows.*)

You're dying to hear the juicy details about my seven demons, I can tell.

(*MAGDALENE fixes her look on a person in the back of the audience and makes a dismissive gesture.*)

No need to raise your hand. The questions are the same wherever I go.

(*MM's eyes grow wide. She mimics questions in an increasingly mocking voice.*)

"What were your demons like?" "Did they have names?" "Did they show up all at once, or one at a time?" "Were you born with demons?" "Did they get inside you on food contaminated with demon spawn?"

(MAGDALENE continues gravely.)

Cruel people say I must have invited the demons in, by committing some horrible sin. I ask you, wasn't being violated by demons enough to suffer, without having these insinuations thrown in my face?

Unfortunately, I can't say for sure that I *didn't* bring them on myself. I simply don't know when, or how, or why the demons entered me. All my memories of the past and all my dreams for the future were kicked out of my head when the demons moved in.

The only thing left of my existence was the present moment. And that contained nothing but hateful demon voices.

(MAGDALENE delivers the following lines in voices of different tone, pitch, and loudness, with attitude and gestures to match the sentiment expressed by each demon—beguiling, commanding, grating, chastising, etc. An undertone of seductive evil should be conveyed in each one.)

Mary… Don't bow down before God, or anyone else. Where's your pride?

Mary… Grab all the wealth you can. A little cheating and stealing never hurt anyone.

Mary… Men desire you. Why deny yourself the pleasure of their *(a beat)* company? Passion will make you feel alive for a change.

Mary… No one appreciates your hard work. Curl up and sleep the day away… Sleep the week away… Sleep your life away…

Mary… Get a load of that woman's jewels, and clothing, and husband, and mansion, and servants. How does she rate?

Mary... Help yourself to another tasty morsel. Come on, have another, whether you're hungry or not. The next bite will be the one that finally satisfies you.

Mary... It's not fair, the way the world treats you! Let your wrath consume them all!

(shout) Mary!

(guttural sneer) Mary!

(shriek) Mary!

(MAGDALENE groans and claps her hands over her ears. After several seconds she composes herself and looks around the audience before continuing in a normal tone.)

You found that disturbing? Even painful? I apologize. Still, my little outburst was downright civilized compared to the brutality that actually thundered in my head.

Oh, yes, I could turn your genteel ears purple with profanity, and not make the slightest dent in the ungodly vocabulary my demons spewed out. I could shred your eardrums with just a feeble echo of their shrieking.

It never let up, day and night. The simple, common word *(a beat)* "Mary" *(a beat)* was transformed into *(a beat)* an instrument of torture.

The demons dictated every word that came out of *my* mouth, too. And manipulated every movement of my body. Do I need to describe to you how a demon-possessed woman is compelled to act?

(MAGDALENE looks around the audience.)

Well... cram the demons of Greed and Sloth and Lust, and all the rest of them, into one brain *(a beat)* and use your imagination, that's all I'll say.

And does anyone here need to be told how the rest of the human race reacted to the sight of me? Loathing doesn't begin to describe it. Polite society took a *(sweeping arm gesture)* wide detour. *Im*polite society spit in my face and jeered, right along with the demons. "Maaaary!" "Mary *Hag*-dalene!" *(a beat)* And a lot worse, with a few rocks thrown in for good measure. I was the lowest of the low in the world's eyes. And in my own.

(MAGDALENE bows her head for a few moments, then sings "See How Far I Have Fallen." For a non-musical production, skip to the stage directions below the lyrics.)

1. See how far I have fallen, deep into black despair! No ray of hope at all and no answer to my prayer. How did it end this way? I once knew light and freedom. Now darkness rules the day.

2. My innocence was taken, youth stolen by my sin, all tenderness forsaken, hardened by guilt within. Bright dreams were left behind. What power can restore them, bring back my peace of mind?

3. Would this world be, I wonder, better if I were dead? Questions tear me asunder. Fear echoes in my head. Were demons sent by hell to torment me forever, inside my heart to dwell?

4. Memories faintly stirring speak of a God above, one who shows undeserving sinners not hate but love. Could God love me so much, to look on me with mercy, healing me with his touch?

(MAGDALENE's face brightens and her voice gains strength.)

My day of deliverance came at last. Praise God! That was the day Jesus of Nazareth touched my life. Jesus cast out the seven demons and made me whole again.

(MAGDALENE looks around the audience for a moment.)

That sounds simple to you? You think it was just—

(MAGDALENE waves her hand like a magic wand.)

"Out, demons! Boom! You're whole!"

Oh, no. You're forgetting. All the memories and thoughts and dreams of Mary, the innocent girl from Magdala, had been destroyed by the demons.

Think about it. Casting out the demons didn't make me whole. It *left* a hole. A silent ... empty ... hole.

(MAGDALENE pauses for three full seconds, looking at the audience, making eye contact, before continuing quietly.)

Did you know that silence can be deafening? Oh, yes. Paralyzing ... Terrifying ... Even a silence that lasts only an instant.

But when that instant ended—

(MAGDALENE grows increasingly animated.)

How can I describe it? Into that awful void there flowed a sort of warmth, like a voice ... a tranquil, beautiful, all-knowing voice, calling my name in a language I'd never heard, and couldn't speak, but understood instinctively. No consonants were articulated, no vowels. Yet somehow, this voice was calling my name ... *(sweetly)* "Mary ..."

Once again, that simple, common word was transformed. This time, into a term of *(a beat)* supreme endearment.

(MAGDALENE delivers the following seven phrases tenderly and expressively.)

Mary ... You are precious in my sight.

Mary ... I know you inside and out.

Mary ... Be at peace; your sins are forgiven.

Mary ... In my strength, you can do all good things.

Mary ... I will keep you safe.

Mary ... I will satisfy the cravings of your soul.

Mary ... I love you.

(MM's voice grows animated.)

I felt Jesus summoning my heart into union with his, filling the void inside me with love, restoring my abused soul, re-creating what it meant to be *(a beat)* Mary Magdalene. Making me *(a beat)* truly whole.

(MAGDALENE resumes her matter-of-fact manner.)

Oh, I could go on all night about that awesome experience, but there's more of my story left to tell. I became my savior's disciple. I accompanied Jesus all over the countryside, even as far as Jerusalem.

Jesus had quite a few faithful followers. Twelve men made up his closest circle. You probably know them as the apostles. There were other men too, and several women besides me. Susanna. A woman named Salome, the wife of Zebedee—two of her sons, John and James, were apostles.

And of course, Joanna. She was married to the manager of King Herod's household.

(MAGDALENE grins and speaks with relish.)

Yes, Herod. If you know Herod's family history of trying to kill Jesus, you've got to love the irony. Thanks to her husband's salary from Herod, Joanna had money at her disposal, and she used it to serve our Lord.

You see, Jesus took no payment for the work he did. We women who had money of our own took it upon ourselves to provide financial support for Jesus and his ministry.

(MAGDALENE sweeps her eyes over the audience and fixes her gaze on a man in the back of the audience.)

What was *that* face for? *(knowingly)* Ah ... Never you mind *how* I got my money.

(MAGDALENE rolls her eyes.)

Honestly, there's one in every crowd. The Jewish leaders thought the worst, too, when they saw women traveling with Jesus. Whoa! Nothing like a whiff of scandal to spice up a dull day in Galilee! *(a beat)* Especially when we passed through areas where the townsfolk remembered Mary *Hag*-dalene.

From time to time, even the apostles would let drop a comment or a nasty look. Yes, there was definitely an undercurrent of jealousy.

(MAGDALENE makes elbowing motions.)

The twelve were constantly jockeying for the Master's favor, and they weren't above listening to ugly rumors about my special relationship with Jesus.

(wistfully) I didn't even try to explain to them about the voice of Jesus in my heart. I was afraid they'd twist that into something shameful.

You want to know the real shame? They could have heard the same sweet call in their own hearts, if they hadn't been so preoccupied with the voices of the world.

(MAGDALENE makes eye contact with the audience.)

Perhaps you have the same problem?

Be that as it may. I figured, if a pack of raving demons couldn't stand between me and Jesus, neither would anyone else. So I just kept my eyes on the Lord.

(MAGDALENE smiles.)

And what a joy he was to watch! I wish all of you could have been there to see Jesus teach and heal. Every day was more amazing than the last. Everything he said and did showed an authority that stopped the Scribes and Pharisees right in their tracks.

Yet he had an endless supply of compassion for the most wretched outcasts. I loved him for that.

Jesus was so gentle with the children who mobbed around him, too. Watching him scoop the little ones into his arms, I couldn't help but think, what a wonderful abba Jesus would be!

My love for Jesus grew stronger and stronger, until it completely possessed me. But not as the demons had possessed me, by force. No. I *freely* gave my mind, my heart, and my soul to Jesus, as a gift of love. Being separated from him was inconceivable.

I remember the night Jesus told us he was going away soon, to a place where we couldn't follow. The apostles were all in a panic, pressing Jesus for an explanation.

I wasn't worried. What difference did it make to *me* where Jesus planned to travel? I loved him and I was going to follow him wherever he went, that's all there was to it.

(*MAGDALENE looks around the audience for several moments, then continues in a sardonic tone.*)

There's that look again. You suspect that's *not* all there was to it. Maybe I gave you too much credit for showing a *well-mannered* interest.

(*MAGDALENE points a finger around the audience.*)

You want to know, is it true that Jesus and I were … lovers? That we had … intimacy?

(*MAGDALENE pauses, then continues matter-of-factly.*)

27

All right. I'll answer those questions. Ooh, that surprised you! But I'm absolutely serious.

(MAGDALENE continues in a powerful voice.)

Then listen! You know that Jesus said: A man has no greater love than to lay down his life for his beloved. *(a pause)* Now, *I'll* tell you this:

(MAGDALENE continues with heartfelt emotion.)

There is no truer lover than a woman standing vigil at a Roman cross, where the man who communes with her very heart and soul *(a beat)* hangs bleeding and gasping ...

(MAGDALENE walks silently to the cross and stands before it, partially turned toward the audience.)

As for intimacy ...

(MAGDALENE speaks the next line slowly and emphatically.)

I tell you, there is no deeper intimacy than witnessing, than *sharing, (a beat)* than *living (a beat)* the unspeakable agony of that beloved man's final hours.

(MAGDALENE turns to face the cross and delivers the following lines very expressively, pausing several seconds for each description to sink in before going on to the next.)

I felt the pain of my Lord's back, ripped by blow after blow of the whip ...

His brow, cut to the bone by a crown of thorns ...

His hands ... the same tender hands that had healed with a touch ... crushed by spikes as he was nailed to the cross ...

His flesh and sinew stretched as the cross was raised, and strained to breaking by his own weight as he hung from it ...

I heard the taunts of passers-by. "You who healed others, heal yourself!" "Come down from the cross if you are the Son of God!" How well I understood the torment inflicted by their mockery!

I heard his voice, ragged from the effort of drawing breath, entrusting his mother to a friend's care and comforting the criminal who hung beside him. Ah, dear Jesus, that was just like you!

Then his hoarse lament, "My God, my God, why have you forsaken me?"

His parched lips and tongue, which had pronounced sweet words of forgiveness... now splashed with sour wine vinegar...

And at the last *(a beat)* his dying cry: *(hoarsely)* "It is finished!"

(longer pause) A soldier's spear pierced his side. A few drops of blood trickled. Then, only water.

Jesus was gone.

(MAGDALENE slowly turns to face audience.)

He'd been right. He was going to a place where I couldn't follow.

(MAGDALENE walks slowly back to center stage.)

Of course, I followed when they took his body down from the cross and carried it to a new tomb in the garden nearby.

(MAGDALENE stands at center stage and faces the audience.)

But the essence of Jesus wasn't there. He was gone from the earth. He was gone *(a beat)* from *me.*

(MAGDALENE echoes Jesus in an anguished voice.)

My Lord, my Lord, why have you forsaken me?

(MAGDALENE covers her face with her hands and stands with her head bent down for several moments. She uncovers her face and raises her head before continuing.)

The next day was the Sabbath, the Jewish day of rest. *(bitterly)* I found no rest in it.

Questions invaded my mind, like demons rushing to take possession.

(MAGDALENE speaks forlornly.)

Where does this leave me?

Why did he leave me?

Who is Mary Magdalene now?

What am I, without Jesus?

Is everything *(a beat)* finished?

(MAGDALENE mournfully sings "O Lord, Whose Touch Once Made Me Whole." For a non-musical production, skip song.)

1. O Lord, whose touch once made me whole, whose love restored my very soul, how can it be that you are gone? Without you, how can I be strong enough to carry on?

2. O Lord, why did you have to leave? Should I be angry? Should I grieve? I was so sure we'd never part. But death has taken you and left me with a hollow heart.

3. O Lord, will I see you again? Does "It is finished" mean the end of everything I thought I knew? Of everything we all believed that you would someday do?

(MAGDALENE stands with bowed head for a few moments, then lifts her head and speaks with quiet resolve.)

The only thing that carried me through those desolate hours was the thought that there was one final service of love I could give to my Lord.

So Sunday, in the early morning mist, I made my way back to the garden with a few of the other women. We carried fragrant burial spices, to anoint the body of Jesus.

As we approached the grave I realized, the soldiers who had been posted to guard it were nowhere in sight.

(MAGDALENE speaks with increasing agitation.)

Odd ... The big stone had already been rolled away from the entrance of the tomb. I ran the last few steps. The tomb was empty! My Lord's body had been taken away! In shock, we hurried back to the house where the apostles were staying, and I told them what I'd seen, but of course they thought my story was hysterical nonsense. Back to the garden we all ran. "Prove me wrong," I wanted to shout. "Please, prove me wrong!"

Peter, then John, entered the tomb. It was empty.

The apostles headed back to the house, debating what this might mean. I stayed in the garden, alone with my grief.

Not quite alone, as it turned out.

A man came up to me. The caretaker, I assumed. I could scarcely make out what he looked like, I was crying so hard. I begged him to tell me where they had taken Jesus.

(MAGDALENE pauses, holding up her hand as if for silence.)

The man answered in a sweet, familiar voice, *(a beat)* "Mary!" I nearly fainted. The man in the garden was my own dear Lord!

When I realized it was neither gardener nor ghost, but Jesus himself, alive, standing beside me, I cried, "Master!" and reached for him.

(MAGDALENE reaches out her hand and closes her eyes while dreamily delivering the next line.)

His touch, for the briefest moment ... !

(MAGDALENE pauses, then speaks matter-of-factly.)

But Jesus slipped away from my embrace, saying, "Don't hold on to me; but go to my brothers. Tell them I'm ascending to the one who is my father and your father, my God and your God."

I didn't know what he meant by that, but I knew all I needed to! My Lord Jesus was alive! Fresh life surged through *me*, too. I ran back to the others with his message, marveling that I, who had brought spices to anoint the dead, had instead found myself anointed, with the balm of pure joy.

Well, my time with you is growing short. So I'll just tell you that Jesus stayed with us for several weeks after that incredible day, teaching and encouraging his disciples for the work ahead of us. Then he ascended to heaven, in our sight. When he departed this time, I was at peace. I understood now that he was leaving me behind, but not forsaking me. Eventually, I would follow.

You see, by his victory over death, the bond of love I shared with Jesus had been elevated to an eternal union ... *(a beat)* with Jesus ... *(a beat)* with his God and our God, his father and our father ... *(MAGDALENE sweeps her arm to encompass the audience)* and with all who accept his offer of salvation.

Because Jesus cast out the seven demons, I was healed. Because my Lord and Savior lives, *(a beat, with a happy glow)* I am transformed!

(Nonmusical production ends here. For a musical production, MAGDALENE sings "Oh, How You Love Me, Jesus.")

(O MIO BABBINO CARO setting)
Oh, how you love me, Jesus! Love beyond understanding! I've never known a love so patient and undemanding. You came not to condemn me, though I deserve no mercy. For all the times I've fallen your tender heart forgives me. Your life you give, that I may live forever and evermore. No love could be more true! Jesus, how I love you!

(HYFRYDOL setting)
Oh, how you love me, Jesus! Love beyond understanding! I have never known a love so patient and undemanding. You came not to condemn me, though I deserve no mercy. For all the times I've fallen your tender heart forgives me. Your life you give, that I may live forever and evermore. No other love could be more true! My dear Jesus, how I love you! Oh, Jesus, how I love you!

THE END

MARY THE MOTHER OF JESUS, TRANSFORMED

Light drama. After Jesus' death, his mother reveals the miraculous circumstances of Jesus' birth to the apostle John. Hearing that Jesus' tomb is empty, Mary immediately understands that her son has risen from the dead, transforming her from giver of earthly life to receiver of eternal life.

CHARACTERS

MAGDALENE ~ Mary Magdalene, a devoted disciple of Jesus. Woman in her twenties or thirties.

MARY ~ Mother of Jesus. Fiftyish woman.

JOHN ~ Beloved apostle of Jesus. Man in his twenties or thirties.

PETER ~ Leader of the apostles of Jesus. Man in his fifties or older.

OTHER DISCIPLES ~ Non-speaking extras, older than John and younger than Peter.

COSTUMES

Simple robes and tunics; a large, plain fabric shawl for MAGDALENE. Optional: Add flaps of torn fabric to the front of clothing and go barefoot to signify mourning.

PROPS

Large wooden table; wooden bench; smaller low bench; large carrying basket with a piece of cloth inside; half a dozen ceramic jars with lids.

SCENE

Dawn, the Sunday after Jesus Christ was crucified. A downstairs room in the house where Jesus' disciples and close family stayed after his death. A table and bench are at center stage facing the audience. An entrance at one side of the stage represents the exterior door of the house. An entrance on the opposite side represents an interior doorway. A large shawl hangs over the small bench, next to the interior doorway. Various jars and a basket are arrayed on the table.

(Mary Magdalene stands with her back to the interior doorway, inspecting the jars and packing them into the basket. After several moments, Mary the mother of Jesus appears in the interior doorway.)

MARY: Mary?

MAGDALENE *(turning, startled)*: Mary! I thought everyone was still in bed.

MARY: I couldn't sleep, thinking about everything that's happened. I heard you rattling around and— *(MARY gestures at the jars and basket.)* But what's all this?

(MAGDALENE draws MARY gently onto the bench behind the table and sits beside her.)

MAGDALENE: Burial spices. I bought them last night. *(JOHN appears in the interior doorway, yawning and running his fingers through his hair. MAGDALENE shows MARY the items in her basket.)* See? The finest fragrances. To anoint the finest man ... *(MARY takes MAGDALENE's hand. JOHN walks up behind the two women, unnoticed.)*

MARY: How generous you are, Mary! I'll get my cloak and go to the garden with you.

(MARY starts to get up and JOHN stops her with his hands on her shoulders.)

JOHN: No, you won't. Mary can handle the arrangements.

MARY *(startled)*: John! As Jesus' mother, I—

JOHN *(interrupting gently but firmly)*: Mary, I respect that you're his mother. But the last thing Jesus asked me to do was to take care of you. Now, you've already been through more than any mother should have to face. Allowing you to tire yourself further wouldn't be very good care, would it?

MAGDALENE: John's right, Mary. The other women will gladly give me whatever help I need. You stay here and rest. *(MAGDALENE finishes bundling her jars, rises, and drapes the shawl across her head and shoulders while JOHN speaks.)*

JOHN *(gravely)*: Yes, rest and pray while you can. There's no telling what turmoil today will bring. The Jewish authorities have had the whole Sabbath to plan their next move.

(MAGDALENE kisses MARY on the cheek and exits through the exterior door.)

MARY *(looking after MAGDALENE)*: Perhaps providing this last service for Jesus will help Mary accept his death.

JOHN: I'm not sure *I* accept it. *(MARY looks questioningly at JOHN.)* Oh, I don't doubt the fact of it. How could I? I was there at the cross. So were you. *(John gestures toward the exterior door.)* Mary Magdalene, too. All three of us witnessed that Jesus ... died.

MARY: Yes.

JOHN: But I can't accept that the whole thing ends! Not this way! All our hopes for kingdom glory. Jesus was supposed to be the Promised One, the Son of God come to save the people of Israel and rule in righteousness! *(passionately)* We can't have been wrong about that!

(JOHN looks hesitantly at MARY, then continues in a rush.)

JOHN: The Lord God himself claimed Jesus as his son! I heard him say it! *(MARY smiles. JOHN misinterprets her smile as one of skepticism.)* I know, it sounds crazy. Oh, you'd understand if you'd seen and heard the incredible things *I* saw and heard.

MARY *(wryly)*: I understand better than you think, John.

JOHN *(caught up in his story)*: It happened just before the group came here to Jerusalem for the Passover. Jesus took me and James and Peter up on a mountaintop to pray. Suddenly we saw Jesus shining as bright as the sun and Elijah and Moses conversing with him. Then we heard the voice of God declaring that Jesus was his son! God himself! When we came down from the mountain, Jesus told the three of us to keep our experience a secret. But now that he's gone ...

MARY *(finishing JOHN's sentence)*: We need to strengthen one another with our first-hand knowledge about who Jesus was.

JOHN: Yes. That's it exactly.

MARY *(thoughtfully)*: Then, the time has come for me to share the secrets I've treasured in my heart for more than thirty years.

JOHN: Secrets about Jesus?

MARY *(patting the bench next to her)*: Sit down, John. Let me tell you some of the incredible things *I* saw and heard. *(MARY pauses as JOHN sits.)* It all began when I was a young girl. With a visit from an angel.

JOHN: An angel!

MARY: I was astonished, too. And terrified. He introduced himself as Gabriel.

JOHN: Gabriel! The Lord God's messenger!

MARY: The angel told me I'd been chosen by God to bear a special child. Now, I'd never been alone with a man and I was old enough to know that was the usual prerequisite for having a baby. So I asked Gabriel how such a thing could be.

JOHN *(aghast)*: You questioned the angel Gabriel?

MARY: He wasn't offended. He assured me that the Lord God was able to bring it about, through the Holy Spirit, that indeed nothing is impossible with God. He said this child would be called the Son of God, the one who would save his people from their sins. I consented, of course. Then Gabriel gave me the child's name. Jesus.

JOHN: So you knew from the start that Jesus was the promised savior.

MARY: Yes.

JOHN: Chosen to be the Messiah's mother! What an incomparable honor!

MARY: You should have heard me singing the Lord's praises after the angel left! How strange and marvelous it was, that the Almighty, the Most High God, would favor an ordinary girl like me, over all the fine women from wealthy, powerful families. What a wonderful sign of God's mercy to the lowly! I would give life to the Son of God! Surely generations to come would call me the most blessed of all women! *(MARY pauses.)* Little did I realize, in that first rush of excitement, what I would be up against.

JOHN: What do you mean?

MARY: I was pledged to marry Joseph, a righteous man. Under the law, he could have had me stoned to death when I turned up pregnant.

JOHN: Oh! Obviously the Lord didn't let that happen.

MARY: He sent an angel to reassure Joseph that it was all right to take me home as his wife, because my child was conceived of the Holy Spirit.

JOHN: Then Joseph also knew that Jesus was sent from God.

MARY: So did my relative Elizabeth. She was elderly and barren, but God blessed her, too. An angel informed her husband that God was going to give them a son.

JOHN: Another angel!

MARY: I traveled to visit Elizabeth when she was six months along. My own pregnancy was too early to show and I hadn't said a word about my condition. Yet Elizabeth knew, the moment she greeted me, that I was carrying the Son of God. She said her baby leaped for joy inside her at the sound of my voice! I've often smiled to recall how John began his ministry of proclaiming the arrival of Jesus while they both were still in the womb.

JOHN: John ... You mean Elizabeth's son—?

MARY *(nodding)*: Grew up to be the one people called John the Baptist.

JOHN: I was one of his disciples before I followed Jesus. John told us that Jesus, not he himself, was the one promised by God. *(a beat)* Did you stay with him and Elizabeth until after Jesus was born?

MARY: No. At that time, the governor decreed that a tax census should be taken. Joseph was descended from the family of David, so he was required to register in David's hometown.

JOHN: Bethlehem.

MARY: Yes. I traveled there with him. What a long, exhausting journey that was! The time for me to give birth was very close when we finally arrived.

JOHN: You must have been relieved to reach the comfort of the inn.

MARY: We certainly were. Until the innkeeper informed us that every room in the place already was occupied. The whole town was bursting with people come to register for the census.

JOHN: What did you do?

MARY: We took shelter in a stable, surrounded by animals. Joseph settled me onto a makeshift bed of hay when my labor began. The pain was excruciating, worse than I'd imagined. But at last it was finished, and I held my firstborn son. Jesus. Giving life to him made all my suffering worthwhile.

JOHN: How strange that the son of God was born in such lowly surroundings!

MARY: Even more surprising was the great fanfare that proclaimed his arrival. There were angels—

JOHN: I should have known!

MARY: Thousands of them filled the night sky, announcing the birth of Jesus and praising God for fulfilling his promise of a savior. Shepherds watching their flocks on the hillsides saw the glorious sight and heard the angels' news. They came running to look for the child and found Jesus, wrapped in swaddling cloths and lying in the manger, just as the angels had told them. What a sight it was, John! Those rough men kneeling on the hay-strewn dirt to worship Jesus. The stable animals looking on like gracious hosts. Joseph standing close by us, as proud and protective as a father could be. (MARY pauses a few moments with eyes closed.) The memory of that night is one of the treasures of my heart. I've pondered it often over the years.

41

JOHN: Incredible!

MARY: When Joseph and I brought the baby to the temple, two elderly servants of God named Simeon and Anna amazed us by loudly thanking the Lord for Jesus, calling him the Christ. *(Mary pauses and grows sad.)* Not everyone was overjoyed by the news of Jesus' birth. When King Herod learned that a child had been born in Bethlehem who would be King of the Jews, he sent his soldiers to slaughter all the little boys in the city. He was determined that not one of them would live to challenge his throne.

JOHN: I've heard stories about that massacre. How did Jesus escape?

MARY: The Lord warned us—

JOHN: Let me guess!

MARY: Yes, an angel told Joseph in a dream to get up at once and take us away because powerful men wanted to harm our child. We fled to Egypt and stayed there until King Herod died.

JOHN: The Lord God protected Jesus.

MARY: Yes, as he always has.

JOHN: No, not always! He didn't send a legion of angels to defend Jesus when he was arrested! He allowed his son to be mocked and tortured and killed, just when he was on the threshold of establishing his kingdom! Why didn't he protect him then? Why?

MARY: It's not necessary for servants to understand their master's plans, John. A faithful servant obeys his master and trusts his promises.

JOHN: Are you suggesting that Jesus' *death* is part of the Lord's kingdom promise? *(He shakes his head.)* How could such a thing be?

MARY: Do you remember the angel Gabriel's answer to that question?

JOHN: "The Lord God is able to bring it about. Nothing is impossible with God." But—

MARY: I know. Jesus' death doesn't make any sense, not to us. But his conception and birth didn't make any sense either.

JOHN (*wryly*): That's true enough.

MARY: Besides, look how generously our master in heaven has favored you and me with personal glimpses of his plans for the future. Shall we repay such extraordinary gifts with anything less than our complete trust?

JOHN (*taking MARY's hand*): Dear woman, your faith gives me new hope. I think Jesus placed you into my care for my benefit more than yours!

(*MARY and JOHN smile at each other for a moment. Then a disturbance is heard at the exterior door and MAGDALENE bursts in, out of breath.*)

MAGDALENE: John! Mary! He's gone!

JOHN: Gone? Who?

MAGDALENE: Jesus! He's gone!

(*JOHN and MARY rise quickly and go to MAGDALENE.*)

MARY: Calm down, Mary. What are you saying?

MAGDALENE: In the garden... The guards were gone and the stone was rolled away... The tomb was empty...

JOHN: Empty!

MAGDALENE: They've taken his body away!

JOHN (*running to the interior doorway, shouting*): Peter! Come here! Quick!

MAGDALENE *(to MARY, who embraces her)*: How could they do such a terrible thing? Wasn't it enough to torture and kill him?

(PETER and OTHER DISCIPLES run into the room.)

JOHN: Who took him? The authorities?

MAGDALENE *(distraught)*: I don't know. I only know the tomb is empty, and Jesus is gone, and I don't know where they've taken him.

PETER: You're not making sense!

(MAGDALENE separates herself from MARY and faces PETER a bit defiantly.)

MAGDALENE: Sense or not, it's the truth. Go see for yourself!

PETER *(to the others)*: Come on!

(MARY sits on the small bench, smiling slightly, as PETER hurries out the exterior door, followed by MAGDALENE and OTHER DISCIPLES. JOHN starts to follow, but turns back to MARY.)

JOHN *(pointing at MARY, sternly but kindly)*: You stay here and rest!

MARY *(serenely)*: I will, John.

JOHN *(surprised and worried by MARY's calmness)*: Do you feel all right? The shock—

MARY *(heartily)*: I couldn't feel better. You go ahead and examine the evidence for yourself.

JOHN: I'll get to the bottom of this, Mary. I promise.

(JOHN runs out the exterior door.)

MARY: I already have the Lord's promise, and he never fails. *(confidently)* My son, Jesus, is the savior of the world.

(MARY stands and faces the audience at front center stage. She looks up to heaven with arms raised.)

44

MARY: Almighty God, one day long ago, I sang your praises for granting me the privilege of giving life to your son, even though I suffered the pains of labor to bring it about. Today, I sing your praises with even greater joy! Today you have granted me, and all the world, salvation through your son! *(MARY closes her eyes.)* My son! I shudder to recall the agony he suffered to bring it about. *(MARY opens her eyes.)* Yes, Lord, I see your plan clearly now. Jesus has been raised, his death transformed into triumph. And I am transformed from giver of earthly life to receiver of eternal life! *(MARY smiles serenely toward the exterior door.)* Yes, John, go investigate that empty tomb. You'll discover the truth it holds, soon enough … *(MARY sits on the small bench.)* As for me, I have new treasures to ponder … *(MARY closes her eyes.)*

THE END

JAMES THE BROTHER OF JESUS, TRANSFORMED

INTERVIEW VERSION

Light drama. James describes how the resurrection of Jesus transformed him from hardened skeptic to ardent believer. Running time is ten to fifteen minutes.

CHARACTERS

INTERVIEWER ~ Host. M/F.

JAMES ~ Guest speaker, a man in his thirties or older.

COSTUMES

Contemporary. Business attire for INTERVIEWER, street clothes for JAMES.

PROPS

Two chairs.

SCENE

The scene can be treated as a Christian talk show or as a guest speaker's presentation during a worship service or other church event. Two chairs at center stage face the audience.

(INTERVIEWER enters.)

INTERVIEWER: Our guest speaker promises to share his personal story of faith in Jesus Christ. Please give a warm welcome to James.

(INTERVIEWER applauds. JAMES enters and shakes hands with INTERVIEWER. They sit.)

INTERVIEWER: James, authorities including Mark and Paul identify you as the brother of Jesus. Is it fair to say you and Jesus were very close to each other when you were growing up?

JAMES: Yes, definitely.

INTERVIEWER: So, you got in on the ground floor when Jesus began his ministry. Were you his top advisor?

JAMES: No. I wasn't his top, bottom, or middle advisor.

INTERVIEWER: Because you were younger than Jesus?

JAMES: Because Jesus didn't want my advice.

INTERVIEWER: Really? But you were one of the twelve apostles. I saw your name on the list.

JAMES: That was a different James. Two different Jameses, actually.

INTERVIEWER: Oh. I'm told that Jesus sent out a group of seventy disciples to preach and heal in his name. Were you ... ?

JAMES: No. I wasn't one of the twelve; I wasn't one of the seventy; I wasn't even one of the bazillion.

INTERVIEWER: The bazillion?

JAMES: The bazillion people who followed Jesus around like sheep. I had no part in Jesus' ministry at all, for the simple reason that I didn't believe he was the Messiah, or the Son of God, or a prophet, or any of that. None of his brothers believed in him.

INTERVIEWER: I don't understand. You said you and Jesus were very close.

JAMES: That was the problem. I knew who Jesus was and where he came from, and it wasn't heaven. He was a regular kid like the rest of us.

INTERVIEWER: Come on! How "regular" could the Son of God be?

JAMES: I have to admit, Jesus always knew his scriptures backwards and forwards... And there was one time when Mary and Joseph had to go pry him out of the temple in Jerusalem. He was so busy schmoozing with the rabbis that he'd missed the caravan home. Otherwise, there was nothing particularly fancy about him.

INTERVIEWER: Then where did he get his authority to preach and heal the sick?

JAMES: That's what everybody in Nazareth wanted to know. After Jesus became an adult and started preaching in the synagogues, you could hear them buzzing. "Isn't that the carpenter's kid? Who does he think he is?"

INTERVIEWER: Who *did* Jesus think he was?

JAMES: Well, one time in our home synagogue, Jesus read a passage from the prophet Isaiah about the promised savior. Then he told the crowd the scripture had come true before their eyes. He might as well have blown a trumpet and yelled, "Look at me! I'm the Messiah!"

INTERVIEWER: How did the people react to that?

JAMES: With an angry uproar, naturally. To make things worse, Jesus made a snappy comment about prophets being dishonored in their home towns. It's a miracle the crowd didn't tear him apart and toss the chunks off a cliff.

INTERVIEWER: Speaking of miracles, what did you think of the ones Jesus performed? Weren't you impressed?

JAMES: If your brother ran around the countryside supposedly raising the dead and forgiving sins, what would *you* think? Our family thought Jesus must be insane. So we acted accordingly.

INTERVIEWER: For example?

JAMES: We heard Jesus wouldn't tear himself away from his adoring fans long enough to get decent meals. That's not healthy. We figured he'd be better off at home where family could take care of him. So we tracked him down to a house in Capernaum—

INTERVIEWER: Which is where?

JAMES: Capernaum? That's a town on the Sea of Galilee, thirty miles or so from Nazareth.

INTERVIEWER: That's a long walk!

JAMES: Sure is! As it turned out, we could have saved our sandal leather.

INTERVIEWER: Jesus refused to go back with you?

JAMES: We never got near enough to ask him to. We sent word that his mother and brothers were waiting outside to see him—

INTERVIEWER: Mary was there, too?

JAMES: Yes. But when we heard the way Jesus answered our message, I wished she wasn't.

INTERVIEWER: Why? What did he say?

JAMES: Jesus asked, "Who are my mother and brothers?" *(grimly)* You should have seen Mary's face.

INTERVIEWER: You're saying Jesus was so far gone he didn't recognize his own family?

JAMES: Oh, he knew us. But he said as far as he was concerned, his "mother and brothers" were the people who listened to God's word and put it into practice.

INTERVIEWER: What did you do next, James?

JAMES: What *could* we do, but hike the thirty miles back home and hope for the best?

INTERVIEWER: Did Jesus cut his ties with the family altogether at that point?

JAMES: No, he came back to Nazareth off and on. He'd show up when it suited him, and leave when it suited him. Like on the Feast of Tabernacles.

INTERVIEWER: That's ... ?

JAMES: The big harvest festival of the Jews.

INTERVIEWER: Okay ...

JAMES: See, Jesus had been teaching in different villages around Galilee for months. It looked like he was staying away from Jerusalem on purpose.

INTERVIEWER: What difference did that make?

JAMES: If you're trying to convince Jews that you're the Messiah, the Holy City is the place to stake your claim, not the hick towns in Galilee.

INTERVIEWER: I see ...

JAMES: Anyway, the Feast of Tabernacles was coming up, and every self-respecting Jew who could ride, walk, or crawl to Jerusalem was expected to be there. A perfect stage for Jesus to display his credentials as Messiah, right?

INTERVIEWER: That seems reasonable.

JAMES: So we—his brothers, I mean—advised Jesus to go with us to Jerusalem, celebrate the feast there publicly, perform miracles in front of the right people ...

INTERVIEWER: I take it Jesus didn't take your advice.

JAMES: Correct. He stayed in Galilee till the rest of the family left for Jerusalem. Then he sneaked into Jerusalem on his own.

INTERVIEWER: Sneaked in? Was he afraid of something?

JAMES *(shrugs)*: He made a cryptic comment about the time not being right for him, or some such thing. The way we saw it, it was just one more example of Jesus doing everything in his own time, in his own way. He didn't even take part in the public observances for the Feast of Tabernacles once he got there.

INTERVIEWER: What did he do instead?

JAMES: Spent all day cooped up in the synagogue, teaching. Is that any way to run a Messiah campaign? I'm telling you, the longer Jesus avoided presenting his Messiah claim to the religious authorities, the more convinced I was that Jesus knew they'd expose him as a fraud.

INTERVIEWER: And did they?

JAMES: Of course not. Oh, they tried to. But they couldn't, because ... he wasn't a fraud after all. It took me a long time to get over my unbelief—and maybe a little bit of sibling jealousy?—but I finally realized the truth.

INTERVIEWER: The truth being ... ?

JAMES: That Jesus is the Messiah, the Christ, the Son of God, the Redeemer—all that and more.

INTERVIEWER: But what changed your mind?

JAMES: Jesus' death and resurrection. Period.

INTERVIEWER: Tell us about that.

JAMES: The family was in Jerusalem for the Passover—another feast when Jews congregate in the Holy City. We got word that Jesus had been arrested and questioned during the night. You already know how he was crucified and died.

INTERVIEWER: Yes ... ?

JAMES: After his body was sealed in a tomb, Mary and my brothers and I went to a house in town where Jesus' disciples were gathered. We stayed there, comforting each other ... praying ... To tell you the truth, we were hiding in a locked upper room in case the authorities decided to come after *us* next.

INTERVIEWER: And then ... ?

JAMES: Then a couple of disciples came to the house with a rumor that Jesus had risen from the dead. Simon Peter and Mary Magdalene claimed they'd seen Jesus alive too. Jesus rising from the dead—that was the most farfetched thing I'd heard yet. But suddenly, Jesus appeared in the room where we were gathered. The doors were still shut and locked. But there he was, standing among us! Alive, in the flesh! He talked to us, invited us to touch him, had us feel the marks of the nails in his hands and the wound in his side where a soldier had pierced him with a spear while he hung on the cross. He opened our eyes—*my* eyes—to what the scriptures said about him, and my doubts disappeared. Truly, he was, and is, the Messiah.

INTERVIEWER: You were an eyewitness in this locked room? Seeing Jesus? Touching Jesus?

JAMES: Yes. And in my encounter with the risen Christ, I was totally transformed, from hardened skeptic to ardent believer. From that point on, my relationship to Jesus was transformed, too, from his earthly brother to his eternal servant. I fell to the floor and worshiped Jesus as my Lord.

INTERVIEWER: Jesus accepted this astounding turn-around?

JAMES: Yes. He never held it against me that my faith was so late in coming. He even trusts me to preach in his name and to work as a leader in the church. I'll always be grateful for that.

INTERVIEWER: And we're grateful to you, James, for joining us today and giving us such a candid testimony.

JAMES: I thought it was important to speak honestly about my years of unbelief, because maybe some of *you* are having a hard time getting past all the reasons the world gives you for not believing in Jesus. You need to know—if *I* can accept the truth, after being so wrong for so long, you can too. Please, don't walk away and put it out of your mind. Place your faith in Jesus—your *complete* faith—and walk with him, all the way to heaven. The longer you wait, the more you stand to lose. Thanks for listening!

THE END

JAMES THE BROTHER OF JESUS, TRANSFORMED

MUSICAL VERSION

Musical comedy/drama. James tries to give his faith testimony on a Christian talk show, but gets drawn into a dispute over his identity as the brother of Jesus Christ. He explains how the resurrection of Jesus made James a believer at last and transformed their relationship into one of servant and Lord.

CHARACTERS

INTERVIEWER ~ TV talk show host who isn't above stirring up controversy to boost ratings. M/F.

JAMES ~ Featured guest, a man in his thirties or older who gamely tries to give his faith testimony.

GUEST #1 ~ Another guest, with a particular theological viewpoint and a penchant for bursting into song when heckling the featured guest. M/F.

GUEST #2 ~ Another guest, who holds the opposite viewpoint. Preferably the same gender as GUEST #1.

MUSICIAN ~ Performs the TV show's theme music and accompanies five short ditties on piano. Is seen but does not speak. MUSICIAN can literally play the piano or can mime playing it while an offstage technician plays pre-recorded music. M/F.

COSTUMES

Contemporary. Business attire for INTERVIEWER, street clothes for guests.

PROPS

Small table; small sofa (or two armless chairs placed side by side); two additional chairs; several sheets of paper; piano (or a prop representing a piano if pre-recorded music is used).

SCENE

Studio of a televised Christian talk show, in the present. The real-life audience serves as the studio audience.

(INTERVIEWER sits behind a small table at center stage, shuffling interview notes. GUEST #1 and GUEST #2 are seated on a sofa to INTERVIEWER's left, facing the audience. An empty chair is on INTERVIEWER's right, facing the audience. MUSICIAN sits at a piano off to one side, facing GUEST #1 and GUEST #2. MUSICIAN plays a few measures of theme music.)

INTERVIEWER: Welcome back to "Christian Witness Tonight." Our next guest promises to share his personal story of faith in Jesus Christ. Please give a nice hand to *(a beat)* James.

(INTERVIEWER stands and applauds. JAMES enters, shakes hands with INTERVIEWER and sits in the chair next to INTERVIEWER. INTERVIEWER sits.)

GUEST #1: James? James what?

JAMES *(puzzled)*: Excuse me?

GUEST #1: You were just introduced as "James." That's not your whole name, is it?

JAMES: Afraid so.

GUEST #2 *(to INTERVIEWER)*: What is he, some kind of mystery guest?

INTERVIEWER: That wasn't our intention.

GUEST #1: Well, it's a mystery to me which James he is.

GUEST #2: Me too. *(GUEST #2 makes rallying gestures to the audience.)* We have a right to know, don't we?

GUEST #1: Yeah!

(Song "Which James?" Asterisks indicate spoken lines.)

>GUEST #1 & GUEST #2: There are way too many James! Why can't they choose different names?

>GUEST #1: James the Less? Or James the Just?

>GUEST #2: Or the son of Alphaeus?

>* INTERVIEWER *(shrugging)*: Don't ask me!

>GUEST #1: How about that other one? Brother of apostle John ...

>GUEST #2: Or the son of Zebedee?

>GUEST #1 *(shaking head)*: They're one man, so that makes ...

>* GUEST #2: Three?

>* GUEST #1 *(counting on fingers, baffled)*: Umm ... I lost count.

>GUEST #2: Luke had mentioned one more James. I don't know his claim to fame.

>GUEST #1: That's at least four James, so far.

>GUEST #1 & GUEST #2: Specify which James you are!

JAMES: All right, all right! I'm James the brother of Jesus.

INTERVIEWER *(flipping through notes)*: You're the brother of Jesus of Nazareth? I don't recall seeing that in your bio.

JAMES: I didn't mention it. I don't like to trade on our relationship. In fact, I'd rather you just call me James the servant of the Lord.

GUEST #2: Oh, no! You're not getting off the hook that easily.

INTERVIEWER: What hook?

GUEST #1 *(to INTERVIEWER)*: Don't get him started.

GUEST #2: Me? *(He points accusingly at JAMES.)* This impostor started it!

JAMES: Now, you wait a minute—

GUEST #1: Don't take it personally, James the whatever-you-are. *(He gestures with his thumb at GUEST #2.)* He denies that *anyone* could be a brother of Jesus.

JAMES: Then forget I said it. Wouldn't have brought it up at all if you two hadn't demanded something to distinguish me from the other Jameses.

GUEST #2: Not good enough!

INTERVIEWER *(baffled)*: Can someone tell me what the issue is here?

JAMES *(sighs)*: It's the Mary thing again.

GUEST #1: The *Virgin* Mary thing.

GUEST #2: Blessed Mary *Ever*-Virgin!

INTERVIEWER *(looking at GUEST #1 and GUEST #2 and pointing at JAMES)*: What's that got to do with him?

GUEST #2: Everything, if he claims to be the brother of Jesus.

(Song "The Mary Thing." Asterisks indicate spoken lines.)

    GUEST #1 & GUEST #2 *(pointing at JAMES)*: When he was a little lad, who did he call Mom and Dad?

    GUEST #1: Is he Mary's nat'ral son?

    GUEST #2: Stepson? Or another one—

    * INTERVIEWER *(puzzled)*: Another what?

GUEST #2: Just another relative in the town where Jesus lived. "Brother" even could refer to some random believer!

* JAMES: Oh, brother!

GUEST #2: Mary never had more kids!

GUEST #1: Gospel writers say she did! God made Mary Joseph's wife.

GUEST #2: She stayed pure all of her life!

GUEST #1: No, she didn't!

GUEST #2: Yes, she did!

(GUEST #1 and GUEST #2 tussle with each other on the sofa.)

JAMES *(wide-eyed)*: Lord, help us ...

INTERVIEWER *(not really displeased with the brawl)*: Please, don't! Stop!

GUEST #1 & GUEST #2 *(straightening up and dusting each other off)*: Sorry ... Very sorry ...

INTERVIEWER *(to James)*: I see why you keep the brother relationship under wraps.

JAMES: That's just it. My testimony keeps getting sidetracked by a debate that doesn't even matter—

GUEST #2: Doesn't matter? *(He turns to INTERVIEWER.)* Are you going to let him sit there and attack one of the most cherished—

JAMES: That's not what I meant! Look, all I'm saying is, who my mother is makes no difference to my faith testimony. So let's leave Mary and Joseph's *(a beat)* marital arrangements *(a beat)* between them and God, okay?

INTERVIEWER: But you're in a unique position—

GUEST #1: Yeah. If you've got proof Mary was your mother, let's settle the issue right here and now.

INTERVIEWER: We'll gladly pay extra for an exclusive.

JAMES: I don't want your money. I told you. I didn't come here to stir up that controversy. Or to settle it, either.

GUEST #2: Because he doesn't have any proof. *(Sniffs loudly.)*

JAMES *(throwing up his hands)*: Believe what you want about my family pedigree, I don't care! My earthly relationship to Jesus isn't important. My spiritual relationship with Jesus is the one I came on the show to testify about. So give me a break, will you?

INTERVIEWER *(gravely, looking straight at audience)*: A man named James. His testimony… right after this break.

(MUSICIAN plays a measure or two of theme music.)

JAMES: That's not the kind of break I meant!

INTERVIEWER: I know, but we have an important earthly relationship with our sponsor.

JAMES: Who's that? The Acme Torch and Pitchfork Company? *(He looks at GUEST #1 and GUEST #2 and shakes his head in disgust.)* Simon Peter warned me about shows like this…

INTERVIEWER: Relax! People love to watch a spirited exchange of religious views.

JAMES: More like hand-to-hand combat!

INTERVIEWER *(patronizingly)*: Look. Controversy is what pulls in the audience. You want an audience listening to your faith message, don't you?

JAMES: Sure, if I ever get a chance to say it.

INTERVIEWER: Don't worry, you will. This is a Christian talk show.

(MUSICIAN plays a few measures of theme music. INTERVIEWER faces the audience.)

INTERVIEWER: Welcome back. I'm here with James, the brother of Jesus. *(At that, GUEST #2 leans forward, ready to start arguing again. INTERVIEWER holds up a hand and gives him a quelling stare.)* However one chooses to define the word "brother." *(GUEST #2 sits back on the couch, satisfied for the moment.)* James, is it fair to say you and Jesus were very close to each other when you were growing up?

JAMES: Yes, definitely.

INTERVIEWER: So, you got in on the ground floor when Jesus began his ministry. Were you his top advisor?

JAMES: No. I wasn't his top, bottom, or middle advisor.

INTERVIEWER: Because you were younger than Jesus?

JAMES: Because Jesus didn't want my advice.

INTERVIEWER: Really? But you were one of the twelve apostles. I saw your name on the list.

JAMES: That was a different James. Two different Jameses, actually. There were a lot of men around named James.

GUEST #1 & GUEST #2 *(in unison)*: I'll say!

(GUEST #1 and GUEST #2 look at MUSICIAN. MUSICIAN plays a few opening notes from "Which James?" but stops when INTERVIEWER makes a throat-cutting gesture.)

INTERVIEWER: You already did, thanks. *(Scans notes.)* Let's see... I'm told that Jesus sent out a group of seventy disciples to preach and heal in his name. Were you...?

JAMES: Nope. I wasn't one of the twelve; I wasn't one of the seventy; I wasn't even one of the bazillion.

INTERVIEWER: The bazillion?

JAMES: The bazillion people who followed Jesus around like sheep. I had no part in Jesus' ministry at all, for the simple reason that I didn't believe he was the Messiah, or the Son of God, or a prophet, or any of that. None of his brothers believed in him.

INTERVIEWER: I don't understand. You said you and Jesus were very close.

JAMES: That was the problem. I knew who Jesus was and where he came from, and it wasn't heaven. He was a regular kid like the rest of us.

GUEST #1: Come on! How "regular" could the Son of God be?

GUEST #2: Yeah...

(Song "Growing Up With the Son of God." Asterisks indicate spoken lines.)

GUEST #1 & GUEST #2: Must have noticed something odd, growing up with the son of God!

GUEST #1: Didn't Jesus give some clue?

GUEST #2: Acting too good to be true?

* JAMES *(shrugging)*: Not really...

GUEST #1: Surely such a special boy wouldn't play with common toys.

GUEST #2: How did Jesus spend his day? Go off on his own to pray?

* JAMES *(nodding)*: Now that you mention it...

GUEST #1: Did he shine in synagogue?

GUEST #2: Did he heal the neighbor's dog?

GUEST #1: Did he have a holy look?

GUEST #2: Memorize the holy book?

JAMES: I have to admit, Jesus always knew his scriptures backwards and forwards ... And there was one time when Mary and Joseph had to go pry him out of the temple in Jerusalem. He was so busy schmoozing with the rabbis that he'd missed the caravan home. Otherwise, there was nothing particularly fancy about him.

INTERVIEWER: Then where did he get his authority to preach and heal the sick?

JAMES: That's what everybody in Nazareth wanted to know. After Jesus became an adult and started preaching in the synagogues, you could hear them buzzing. "Ain't that the carpenter's kid? Who does he think he is?"

INTERVIEWER: Who *did* Jesus think he was?

JAMES: Well, one time in our home synagogue, Jesus read a passage from the prophet Isaiah about the promised savior. Then he told the crowd the scripture had come true before their eyes. He might as well have blown a trumpet and yelled, "Look at me! I'm the Messiah!"

INTERVIEWER: How did the people react to that?

JAMES: With an angry uproar, naturally. To make things worse, Jesus made a snappy comment about prophets being dishonored in their home towns. It's a miracle the crowd didn't tear him apart and toss the chunks off a cliff.

INTERVIEWER: Speaking of miracles, what did you think of the ones Jesus performed? Weren't you impressed?

JAMES: Get real! If your brother ran around the countryside supposedly raising the dead and forgiving sins, what would *you* think?

GUEST #1: I'd think my brother was nuts.

GUEST #2: I've met your brother. He really *is* nuts.

JAMES: Our family thought Jesus must be insane, too. So we acted accordingly.

INTERVIEWER: For example?

JAMES: We heard Jesus wouldn't tear himself away from his adoring fans long enough to get decent meals. That's not healthy. We figured he'd be better off at home where family could take care of him. So we tracked him down to a house in Capernaum—

INTERVIEWER: Which is where?

JAMES: Capernaum? That's a town on the Sea of Galilee, thirty miles or so from Nazareth.

INTERVIEWER: That's a long walk!

JAMES: Sure is! As it turned out, we could have saved our sandal leather.

INTERVIEWER: Jesus refused to go back with you?

JAMES: We never got near enough to ask him to. We sent word that his mother and brothers were waiting outside to see him—

INTERVIEWER: Mary was there, too?

JAMES: Yeah. But when we heard the way Jesus answered our message, I wished she wasn't.

INTERVIEWER: Why? What did he say?

JAMES: Jesus asked, "Who are my mother and brothers?" *(grimly)* You should have seen Mary's face.

INTERVIEWER: You're saying Jesus was so far gone he didn't recognize his own family?

JAMES: Oh, he knew us. But he said as far as he was concerned, his "mother and brothers" were the people who listened to God's word and put it into practice.

GUEST #2 *(triumphantly)*: What did I tell you? Any believer can be called a brother of Jesus!

(GUEST #2 motions to MUSICIAN, who obediently plays a few opening notes from "The Mary Thing" until INTERVIEWER glares and makes the throat-cutting gesture again.)

GUEST #1 *(annoyed, to GUEST #2)*: Give it a rest, will you? I'm trying to listen ...

INTERVIEWER: What did you do next, James?

JAMES: What *could* we do, but hike the thirty miles back home and hope for the best?

INTERVIEWER: Did Jesus cut his ties with the family altogether at that point?

JAMES: No, he came back to Nazareth off and on. He'd show up when it suited him, and leave when it suited him. Like on the Feast of Tabernacles.

INTERVIEWER: That's ... ?

JAMES: The big harvest festival of the Jews.

INTERVIEWER: Okay ...

JAMES: See, Jesus had been teaching in different villages around Galilee for months. It looked like he was staying away from Jerusalem on purpose.

INTERVIEWER: What difference did that make?

JAMES: Look, if you're trying to convince Jews that you're the Messiah, the Holy City is the place to stake your claim, not the hick towns in Galilee.

INTERVIEWER: I see ...

JAMES: Anyway, the Feast of Tabernacles was coming up, and every self-respecting Jew who could ride, walk, or crawl to Jerusalem was expected to be there. A perfect stage for Jesus to display his credentials as Messiah, right?

INTERVIEWER: That seems reasonable.

JAMES: So we—his brothers, I mean—advised Jesus to go with us to Jerusalem, celebrate the feast there publicly, perform miracles in front of the right people ...

INTERVIEWER: I take it Jesus didn't take your advice.

JAMES: Correct. He stayed in Galilee till the rest of the family left for Jerusalem. Then he sneaked into Jerusalem on his own.

INTERVIEWER: Sneaked in? Was he afraid of something?

JAMES (shrugs): He made a cryptic comment about the time not being right for him, or some such thing. The way we saw it, it was just one more example of Jesus doing everything in his own time, in his own way. He didn't even take part in the public observances for the Feast of Tabernacles once he got there.

INTERVIEWER: What did he do instead?

JAMES: Spent all day cooped up in the synagogue, teaching. Is that any way to run a Messiah campaign? I'm telling you, the longer Jesus avoided presenting his Messiah claim to the religious authorities, the more convinced I was that Jesus knew they'd expose him as a fraud.

GUEST #2: I've had enough of this fellow's insinuations.

GUEST #1: Whew! He wasn't kidding when he said he didn't believe in Jesus.

INTERVIEWER (gravely, looking straight at the audience): James and Jesus ... Brotherly love? Or brotherly hate? We'll find out ... after this break.

(MUSICIAN plays a measure or two of theme music. INTERVIEWER holds a smarmy smile for a moment, then turns angrily on JAMES.)

INTERVIEWER: You're a good one to talk about fraud!

JAMES: What's that supposed to mean?

INTERVIEWER: You were booked to give a first-person story about your Christian faith, but all you've talked about is why you *don't* believe in Jesus!

JAMES: Now, hold on—

INTERVIEWER: No, *you* hold on! A spicy bit of controversy is one thing. Appearing on "Christian Witness Tonight" under false pretenses is something else.

GUEST #1 & GUEST #2 *(in unison)*: Yeah!

(Song "Pro or Con?" Asterisks indicate spoken lines.)

> GUEST #1 & GUEST #2: First you claim you're family, then speak like an enemy.
>
> GUEST #1: Are you calling Christ a fraud?
>
> GUEST #2: Do you call him Son of God?
>
> * JAMES *(holding up a hand)*: I was just getting to that...
>
> GUEST #1: "Spiritual relationship" rolled so sweetly from your lip.
>
> GUEST #1 & GUEST #2: Are you trying to deceive us about what you believe?
>
> * JAMES *(anxiously)*: I can explain!
>
> GUEST #2: Better make your meaning clear.
>
> GUEST #1: Nice and loud so we can hear!
>
> GUEST #2: Which side are you really on?
>
> GUEST #1 & GUEST #2: Are you pro or are you con?

GUEST #2: He's obviously a pro at pulling a con. *(Sniffs.)*

JAMES: That was uncalled for!

(MUSICIAN plays a few measures of theme music.)

INTERVIEWER *(looking directly at the audience)*: We're back with James, a *(a beat)* self-proclaimed brother of Jesus of Nazareth, and apparently *not* a Christian believer as he led us all to believe.

JAMES *(exasperated)*: Let me explain! *(JAMES turns to the audience.)* I'm sorry. I guess I misled you, but not on purpose. And not the way these guys think.

GUEST #1 *(dismissively)*: More double-talk.

JAMES: Bear with me, please. Obviously I gave the wrong impression by talking too much about the time when I *didn't* believe in Jesus. I wanted to show you how growing up with Jesus was actually *(a beat)* an obstacle to my finding faith. There were so many reasons to be skeptical. Maybe a little brotherly jealousy at work, too. *(He smiles toward GUEST #1 and GUEST #2.)* However one chooses to define the word "brotherly." *(He turns back toward the audience.)* But that's all in the past. I wanted you to see where I'm coming from, because maybe *you're* having a hard time getting past all the reasons the world gives you for not believing in Jesus. You need to know—if *I* can accept the truth, after being so wrong for so long, you can too.

INTERVIEWER: Your truth being ... ?

JAMES: *The* truth being that Jesus is the Messiah, the Christ, the Son of God, the Redeemer—all that and more. *(JAMES looks defiantly at INTERVIEWER, GUEST #1, and GUEST #2.)* Is that clear enough?

INTERVIEWER *(dissatisfied)*: Yes, as far as it goes. But you've left out the most important part.

GUEST #1: Yeah. After all your reasons for not believing in Jesus—

GUEST #2 *(suspiciously)*: What changed your mind?

JAMES *(matter-of-factly)*: Jesus' death and resurrection. Period.

INTERVIEWER: Tell us about that.

JAMES: Gladly! The family was in Jerusalem for the Passover—another feast when Jews congregate in the Holy City. We got word that Jesus had been arrested and questioned during the night. You already know how he was crucified and died.

GUEST #1 & GUEST #2 *(leaning forward)*: Yes ... ?

JAMES: After his body was sealed in a tomb, Mary and my brothers and I went to a house in town where Jesus' disciples were gathered. We stayed there, comforting each other ... praying ... To tell you the truth, we were hiding in a locked upper room in case the authorities decided to come after *us* next.

GUEST #1 & GUEST #2 *(leaning forward)*: And then ... ?

JAMES: Then a couple of disciples came to the house with a rumor that Jesus had risen from the dead. Simon Peter and Mary Magdalene claimed they'd seen Jesus alive too. Jesus rising from the dead—that was the most farfetched thing I'd heard yet. But suddenly, Jesus appeared in the room where we were gathered. The doors were still shut and locked. But there he was, standing among us! Alive, in the flesh! He talked to us, invited us to touch him, had us feel the marks of the nails in his hands and the wound in his side where a soldier had pierced him with a spear while he hung on the cross. He opened our eyes—*my* eyes—to what the scriptures said about him, and my doubts disappeared. Truly, he was, and is, the Messiah.

INTERVIEWER: You were an eyewitness in this locked room?

GUEST #1: Seeing Jesus?

GUEST #2: Touching Jesus?

JAMES: Yes. And in my encounter with the risen Christ, I was totally transformed, from hardened skeptic to ardent believer. From that point on, my relationship to Jesus was transformed, too, from his earthly brother to his eternal servant. I fell to the floor and worshiped Jesus as my Lord.

INTERVIEWER: Jesus accepted this astounding turn-around?

JAMES: Yes. Jesus never held it against me that my faith was so late in coming. He even trusts me to preach in his name and to work as a leader in the church. I'll always be grateful for that. And, I'm grateful to "Christian Witness Tonight" for giving me this opportunity to share my testimony with all the other confirmed skeptics out there. *(JAMES rolls his eyes and grins.)* Finally!

INTERVIEWER: Well, there you have it. *(He looks solemnly at audience.)* James. Transformed from brother to believer, by the risen Christ.

(Song "All That Counts." Asterisks indicate spoken lines.)

GUEST #2: James's story does ring true.

GUEST #1: I believe him.

INTERVIEWER: I do, too.

GUEST #1 & GUEST #2: Let's agree to disagree on the fellow's family tree.

* JAMES: That's the spirit!

JAMES, GUEST #1 & GUEST #2: All that counts is having faith.

JAMES: Even if you find it late.

JAMES, GUEST #1 & GUEST #2: We believe the truth is this: Jesus, our Redeemer, lives!

* INTERVIEWER: Any closing remarks?

JAMES, GUEST #1 & GUEST #2: We don't care what else you say, please describe us in this way:

ALL: Servants of the Living God and of Jesus Christ, our Lord!

INTERVIEWER: That's our show. Good night, everyone!

(MUSICIAN plays theme music as the others stand and bow to each other and wave to the audience.)

THE END

JOHN THE APOSTLE, TRANSFORMED

Dramatic monologue. Shortly after receiving the news that his brother, James, has been executed by King Herod, visiting preacher John the Apostle describes how his family's hopes for special honors in the coming kingdom of God were transformed by the resurrection of Jesus.

CHARACTER

JOHN ~ Beloved apostle of Jesus. A man in his thirties or forties.

COSTUME

Simple robe/tunic, sandals.

PROPS

Simple chair and table; scroll-style letter (rolled sheets of paper tied with string).

SCENE

Lecture hall or meeting room, the year 44 AD. Chair and table are center stage, facing the audience. The letter is on the table.

(JOHN enters and begins to speak.)

Good evening. This is the year 44 AD, eleven years after Jesus Christ was crucified. You've gathered in a small meeting hall somewhere, doesn't matter where, to hear a traveling preacher named John. Some call me John the Apostle or John the Evangelist.

(JOHN notices the letter and hastily opens it.)

It's a letter from my mother. Excuse me ... *(frowning)* We recently heard some terrible news, so I'm anxious to see what Mother has to say ...

(JOHN reads aloud.)

"My dear son, I'm writing to offer you what comfort I can, as we mourn our beloved James. The believers here have been a great consolation to me. I overheard one say that death by the sword is quick, so I cling to the hope that James suffered very little."

(JOHN lowers the letter and speaks to the audience.)

Death by the sword. A polite way of saying that James was beheaded. That was the news we received. King Herod Agrippa executed my brother.

You might wonder why anyone would want to kill a godly man like James. This was power politics, in the Herod family tradition.

Do you remember Herod the so-called Great? He ordered his soldiers to slaughter all the babies in Bethlehem—hoping to get rid of the child Jesus in the process—because he was afraid Jesus would pose a threat to his throne someday. That Herod was our Herod Agrippa's grandfather.

Herod Agrippa also had an uncle called Herod Antipas. He's the one who beheaded John the Baptist and presided over the crucifixion of Jesus.

Now, Herod Agrippa has been appointed King of Palestine by the Roman emperor. He knows he'll soon be the *former* King of Palestine if he fails to keep his Jewish subjects happy. The surest way to keep the Jews happy is to persecute the Christian church. My brother James refused to stop preaching about Jesus. So Herod Agrippa murdered him.

(JOHN reads aloud.)

"I suppose I knew our Lord's apostles couldn't escape persecution forever. But it was very hard to learn that my own son was the first to fall."

(JOHN lowers the letter and looks off into space, nodding.)

Yes, James is the first of the twelve to die a martyr's death ...

(JOHN looks at the audience.)

Strange as this may sound, Mother and I are grateful to God for granting my brother the high honor of being the first apostle to enter the kingdom. There's not a doubt in my mind—James is seated in glory with the Lord right now. Exactly as we requested so long ago ...

Let me tell you how that request came about.

Back probably twelve or thirteen years ago, James and I were working in a small fishing business on the Sea of Galilee with our father, Zebedee. Jesus of Nazareth came along and invited us to be his disciples. You may have heard how James and I dropped everything to follow Jesus. But did you know my mother came along, too?

(JOHN smiles and speaks affectionately.)

She took care of our day-to-day needs while we toured the countryside with Jesus. Pretty spunky, don't you think? Especially considering the *(a beat) interesting* characters who surrounded Jesus wherever we went.

One day, after James and I had been disciples of Jesus a couple of years or more, our group was traveling to Jerusalem to celebrate the Passover there. That was our last trip with Jesus, though we didn't realize it at the time.

Along the way, there had been quite a bit of haggling among our Lord's inner circle of twelve disciples. The apostles, as people call us nowadays. We were arguing about which of us was the greatest, who was in line for the highest honors, that sort of thing.

Jesus had already designated Simon, one of my family's fishing partners, as the lead apostle. That was understandable, Simon being the oldest of the twelve.

Not to be outdone, Mother decided to make sure James and I got high-ranking positions too. She watched until Jesus was alone, then took us over to him. We knelt in front of Jesus, to show we had a serious favor to beg.

Mother did the talking. She asked Jesus for his assurance that one of her two sons would sit at his right hand and the other at his left, when Jesus came into the glory of his kingdom.

So you understand exactly what Mother was requesting, I should say a few words about the kingdom promise. Like many generations of faithful Jews before us, we'd been brought up hearing about God's promise to send us a savior who would establish a new, righteous kingdom.

As far as I was concerned, with the country being squashed under the thumb of the Roman Empire and ruthless politicians like King Herod Agrippa running the local government, it was high time for the savior to show up.

Some of us were convinced that Jesus of Nazareth was the one to do it. Seize power! Kick out the Romans! Set our people free, once and for all! Then Jesus could claim the throne, establish his righteous kingdom, and reign in glory.

(JOHN pauses and raises his eyebrow.)

With me and James sitting regally on either side of him. That was my family's picture of the kingdom, anyway. And that's what we asked Jesus to promise.

Pretty presumptuous, right? To be fair, though, it's not as if we plucked our grand aspirations out of thin air. Jesus had already singled me out as a close friend whom he loved —a younger brother, for all intents and purposes.

More than that, he had revealed glimpses of his coming glory to James and me, as well as to Simon. For example, Jesus allowed *us*, and nobody else, to witness his bringing Jairus's dead daughter back to life. Three fishermen from Galilee don't get a privilege like that every day!

The most spectacular privilege had to be the time he took Simon, James, and me up on a mountaintop to pray. Right before our eyes, Jesus turned shining white, like the sun. The prophets Moses and Elijah appeared and chatted with Jesus like old friends. We even heard the voice of God! Amazing!

To top it off, Jesus gave the three of us special nicknames. He called Simon "Peter"—the Rock. James and I were the "Sons of Thunder."

All in all, we knew we were special to Jesus. So why not ask for special treatment?

Back to James and me on our knees… When Jesus heard the favor we wanted, he told us we didn't know what we were asking. I looked out the corner of my eye at James, and he gave a little shrug. Sitting next to Jesus in glory seemed clear-cut to us.

Jesus asked, "Are you able to drink the cup I drink?" Right off, I said, "Yes, Lord, of course we are!"

Then Jesus asked, "And can you be baptized the same way I'm baptized?" I thought Jesus wanted to dunk us in the river, like John the Baptist had dunked *him*. No problem. What's a little water to men who've sailed through storms on the Sea of Galilee?

Jesus listened to our hasty assurances. He agreed, with a peculiar gleam in his eye, that we would indeed drink from his cup and share his baptism.

When I heard that, I was all set to have the names "James" and "John" carved on those prime seats in the kingdom. Only question in my mind was which one of us would get the seat on Jesus' right, and which one the seat on his left.

But Jesus squelched the whole idea. He told us he didn't have authority to assign the places of honor at his side. Those places, he said, belonged to the ones for whom they'd been prepared by his Father.

That looked like the end of that. James and I got up off our knees and slumped away.

Mother said nothing more to Jesus about it. But she was not deterred. She pointed out to us privately that Jesus hadn't actually said we *weren't* the ones those places of honor had been prepared for.

(JOHN shakes his head and smiles wryly.)

Hey, she was thrilled that Jesus threw in the cup and baptism as a bonus!

(JOHN shakes his head sadly.)

Poor Mother ... Her faith has proved right, for James at least. But I'm getting ahead of myself.

As you can imagine, the other apostles were angry when they found out James and I had gone fishing for favors. Jesus heard the ruckus and sat us all down for a lecture.

He explained that the way to be great in his kingdom is by becoming the servant of all, not by lording it over everyone else. They all glared at James and me when Jesus said that, but I was too intrigued by his lesson to care.

See, it struck me that Jesus didn't just say, "*You disciples* have to be like servants." No. He told us that *he himself* came to serve, not to be served. He said he would even give up his own life, in atonement for many people!

That was unheard of! The heir to the new kingdom was willing to be sacrificed as a sin offering?

Yet, looking back, that wasn't the first time Jesus had said such things. In fact, shortly before Mother, James, and I went to see Jesus, he had warned us twelve—plainly!—that he was going to be betrayed to the chief priests and condemned to death when we got to Jerusalem.

He gave details, right down to the flogging, the mockery, the crucifixion. But we always went right back to basking in the sunshine of miracles and love and forgiveness and dreams of kingdom victory ... paying little or no heed to the *dark* things Jesus foretold.

After the kingdom lecture, I was relieved to find that Jesus didn't hold our throne request against us. He continued to give me special commissions, like preparing the room for our Passover meal when we arrived in Jerusalem.

Oh, there are a million things I could tell you about that Passover week. I'd be here all night just skimming the surface, so much happened.

At our last supper, I sat next to Jesus, leaning so close that I could feel the emotion trembling through his body as he lifted the cup ... gave thanks ... and told all of us to drink from it.

I was the first to drink. I held the cup in both my hands and savored the wine and the honor, feeling a nice warm glow from both ...

Until the rest of his words sank in. He called the cup his blood of a new covenant. He said it would be shed on behalf of many for the forgiveness of sins.

There were those dark predictions again! I quickly passed the cup to the next man.

After supper, Jesus led us to an olive grove across the valley. He took aside James, Simon, and me—the three special ones—and told us to be on the alert while he prayed.

The air was so quiet and sweet... My belly was full of food and wine... We'd had a long day...

Next thing I knew, Jesus was shaking me awake. He urged us again to pray with him. I should have realized that something was up, but do you think I could keep my eyes open?

Well, I came to, quick enough, when a crowd of soldiers and officials tramped into the grove carrying swords and clubs. With that *(a beat)* traitor, Judas Iscariot, in the lead.

One of the chosen twelve! I was absolutely stunned.

Judas kissed Jesus. Betraying him with traces of wine from the shared cup still on his lips ...

Simon Peter jumped up with a sword in his hand and started swinging, but Jesus wasn't having any of that. He said the time had come for him to drink the cup of suffering his Father had given him. Then he calmly allowed the mob to tie his hands like a criminal, and they dragged him away.

I recalled the strange look on his face when he told James and me that, yes, we would drink from the same cup he drinks from. Now I knew. It was his cup of suffering we were destined to share.

I tasted a tiny drop from that cup there in the garden ...

(JOHN grows more emotional as he speaks.)

Sipped a bit more while Jesus was questioned and mocked ...

Drank deeper when he was scourged ...

Choked down a big gulp when he was crucified ...

And drained it, down to the last bitter dregs, as I watched him ... cry out ... and die ...

(JOHN pauses to compose himself.)

I'll never forget that scene. Jesus' mother, Mary Magdalene, a handful of our Lord's other friends, all torn between numbness and agony. None of my fellow apostles showed their faces. I found out later that Judas Iscariot had done away with himself. The rest were in hiding.

(JOHN smiles.)

Guess who *did* stick around.

(JOHN nods and taps the letter with his finger.)

My mother. Salome, the wife of Zebedee. Even when her kingdom dreams were nailed to a Roman cross, that dear, spunky woman stood by me and our Lord. Still undeterred ...

And Mother was right to keep the faith. The kingdom promise wasn't canceled at the cross. It was fulfilled ... at the tomb.

Which brings me to the speech I came here to give in the first place.

I travel all over the map to preach this message, because I know how important it is, for *your* sakes, that you hear it and believe.

With my own two eyes, I saw the events I'm about to relate. I know they are true.

On the third day after Jesus was crucified, early in the morning, Mary Magdalene came running to the house where the remaining apostles were holed up. She claimed she'd been to the tomb where the body of Jesus had been buried, and it was vacant. His body was gone, she said. That didn't make any sense, so we hurried to check it out for ourselves.

I outran the other apostles and saw, sure enough, the big round stone that sealed the opening of the tomb had been rolled off to one side. I waited for Simon Peter to go inside first, since he was our leader. To tell you the truth, it was all I could do not to elbow the old fellow out of the way, that's how anxious I was to find out what was going on!

Finally I got my turn to examine the tomb. The burial linens I'd seen wrapped around our Lord's body were folded in a nice neat pile on the stone slab, where his head had lain. Otherwise, the tomb was empty. Jesus was gone.

That's when a hint of the truth came back to me. Those times when Jesus foretold his suffering and death? He'd always added something else. He'd always said he would rise again on the third day.

This had to be it! The third day wasn't some abstract metaphor. His rising wasn't just another parable. Jesus had told us, literally, what was going to happen.

I began to understand, as I crouched there in the empty tomb. In that one transforming moment, I saw, and I believed.

Yes, Jesus Christ *was* the one sent by God to save his people, once and for all, and establish a new, righteous kingdom, as we had hoped. But he did it in his own, unheard-of way. By suffering and dying, as a willing sacrifice.

Not your idea of kingdom glory? Wasn't mine, either, before I saw that empty tomb. But I finally got it.

The victory Jesus had to win wasn't over the Roman army, or the religious authorities, or ruthless politicians. He defeated something much bigger. Death itself!

He rose from the dead on the third day, exactly as he said he would, and he lives—right now, today—on the throne of the ultimate righteous kingdom. The kingdom of heaven.

If you and I place our faith in Jesus above our old, selfish ambitions, we stand to share in his triumph over death. That's right. Jesus taught that the one who seeks to save his own life will lose it. But the one who surrenders his life for the sake of Jesus, as my brother James did, will save it.

My family's picture of kingdom glory changed completely when we witnessed the resurrection of Jesus. And now, that portrait has been updated to include James, the son of Zebedee, the "Son of Thunder," sitting close to Jesus, the Son of God. *(a beat)* Just as our mother requested.

I pray that someday we'll see *you* in the glory of that heavenly kingdom. Amen.

THE END

Songs

MARY MAGDALENE'S MUSIC

Three optional songs are provided for the monologue "Mary Magdalene, Transformed." They call for an expressive soloist with vocal ability. Slow tempo, light accompaniment, and sensitive phrasing will create a dramatic vocal performance to touch the audience's hearts.

"See How Far I Have Fallen" is set to a simplified version of the haunting melody ES IST EIN ROS, familiar from the carol "Lo, How a Rose E'er Blooming."

"O Lord, Whose Touch Once Made Me Whole" is set to Albert L. Peace's tune ST. MARGARET, which appears in many hymnals with the text titled "O Love That Wilt Not Let Me Go."

"Oh, How You Love Me, Jesus" is set to the melody of "O Mio Babbino Caro," the short, tender aria from Puccini's opera *Gianni Schicchi*. A basic lead sheet is provided here for the key of F. If a more sophisticated arrangement or a lower key is desired, you can obtain your choice of sheet music for "O Mio Babbino Caro" and substitute the words of "Oh, How You Love Me, Jesus," syllable for syllable.

A less demanding alternate setting for "Oh, How You Love Me, Jesus" also is provided. It is adapted from the Welsh tune HYFRYDOL *(huh-vruh-dol)*, which has been used as the setting for a number of hymn texts, including "Come, Thou Long-Expected Jesus" and "Love Divine, All Loves Excelling." This tune ends Mary Magdalene's story on a heartfelt note of gladness. The accompaniment draws upon both the original harmonization and a simplified version in the 1906 *English Hymnal.*

See How Far I Have Fallen

Words by Linda Bonney Olin, 2013
Music from Alte Catholische Geistliche Kirchengesang,1599;
arranged by Michael Praetorius, 1609; adapted by Linda Bonney Olin, 2013

(MARY MAGDALENE)

1. See how far I have fall - en, deep
2. My in - no - cence was tak - en, youth
3. Would this world be, I won - der, bet -
4. Mem - o - ries faint - ly stir - ring speak

in - to black de - spair! No ray of hope at
sto - len by my sin, all ten - der - ness for -
ter if I were dead? Ques - tions tear me a -
of a God a - bove, one who shows un - de -

all and no an - swer to my prayer. How
sak - en, hard - ened by guilt with - in. Bright
sun - der. Fear ech - oes in my head. Were
serv - ing sin - ners not hate but love. Could

did it end this way? I once knew light and
dreams were left be - hind. What pow - er can re -
de - mons sent by hell to tor - ment me for -
God love me so much, to look on me with

free - dom. Now dark - ness rules the day.
store them, bring back my peace of mind?
ev - er, in - side my heart to dwell?
mer - cy, heal - ing me with his touch?

O Lord, Whose Touch Once Made Me Whole

Words by Linda Bonney Olin, 2013
Music by Albert L. Peace, 1884

(MARY MAGDALENE)

1. O Lord, whose touch once made me whole,
2. O Lord, why did you have to leave?
3. O Lord, will I see you a - gain?

whose love re-stored my ver - y soul,
Should I be an - gry? Should I grieve?
Does "It is fin - ished" mean the end

6

how can it be that you are
I was so sure we'd nev - er
of eve - ry - thing I thought I

8

gone?_____ With - out you, how can I be
part._____ But death has tak - en you and
knew?_____ Of eve - ry - thing we all be -

10

strong e - nough to car - ry on?
left me with a hol - low heart.
lieved that you would some - day do?

Oh, How You Love Me, Jesus (O MIO BABBINO CARO)

Words by Linda Bonney Olin, 2013
Music by Giacomo Puccini, 1918; adapted by Linda Bonney Olin, 2013

(MARY MAGDALENE)

Oh, how you love me, Je-sus! Love be-yond un-der-stand-ing! I've nev-er known a love so pa-tient and un-de-mand-ing. You came not to con-demn me, though I de-serve no mer-cy. For

all the times I've fall - en your ten-der heart for -

gives me. Your life you give, that I may live for-

ev - er_____ and ev - er - more.

No love could be more true! Jesus, how I love__ you!

Oh, How You Love Me, Jesus (HYFRYDOL)

Words by Linda Bonney Olin, 2013
Music by Rowland Prichard, 1830; adapted by Linda Bonney Olin, 2013

(MARY MAGDALENE)

Oh, how you love me, Je - sus!

Love be-yond un - der - stand - ing!

I have nev - er known a love so

patient and un - de - mand - ing. You

came not to con - demn me, though I de -

serve no mer - cy. For all the

times I've fall - en your ten-der heart for -

gives me. Your life you give, that I may

live for - ev - er and ev - er - more.

No oth-er love could be more true!

My dear Je - sus, how I love you!

Oh, Je-sus, how I love you!

JAMES'S MUSIC

Five ditties are an integral part of the musical version of the dramatic comedy "James the Brother of Jesus, Transformed." Cast members do not need legitimate singing voices, but they must be able to articulate their lyrics clearly, with personality, and keep up with the snappy pace of musical repartee. To make their task easier, all five ditties are set to the same simple tune, adapted from the familiar song "Up on the House Top" by Benjamin Hanby.

Sheet music for each ditty is provided with words and melody for the actors, laid out on facing pages. Character labels above the staff identify which character(s) sing the lyrics in that measure. To fit the space, lyrics for Guest #1 and Guest #2 are labeled "G1" and "G2." Words that are spoken, not sung, are printed above the staff, next to the character label.

For the actors' convenience in rehearsals and Readers Theatre productions, the lyrics of the five ditties are printed in the script, too.

Sheet music without lyrics for the accompanist's use follows on separate pages. The accompaniment can be played live by the MUSICIAN character or pre-recorded for playback during the performance. Either way, be sure to extend the empty measures long enough for the speaking characters to deliver their lines.

Stage directions for this play call for short bits of theme music to play before and after each commercial break in the fictional TV show. Any suitable music clip can serve that purpose.

Which James?

Words by Linda Bonney Olin, 2013
Music by Benjamin Hanby, 1864; adapted by Linda Bonney Olin, 2013

(G1, G2, INTERVIEWER)

G1 & G2:
There are way too man-y James!

Why can't they choose dif - ferent names?

G1:
James the Less? Or James the Just?

G2:
Or the son of Al - phae - us?

INTERVIEWER: Don't ask me!

G1:
How a-bout that oth-er one? Broth-er of a -

pos-tle John... Or the son of Zeb-e-dee?

G1:
G2: Three?

They're one man, so that makes...

G1: *(counting on fingers)* Umm... I lost count...

G2:

Luke had men-tioned one more James.

I don't know his claim to fame.

G1:

That's at least four James, so far.

G1 & G2:

Spec - i - fy which James you are!

The Mary Thing

Words by Linda Bonney Olin, 2013
Music by Benjamin Hanby, 1864; adapted by Linda Bonney Olin, 2013

(ALL)

G1 & G2:

When he was a lit-tle lad,

who did he call Mom and Dad?

G1:

Is he Mar-y's nat'-ral son?

G2:

Step-son? Or an-oth-er one...

INTERVIEWER: Another what?

G2:

Just an-oth-er rel-a-tive in the town where

14
Je - sus lived. "Broth - er" e - ven
16
could re - fer to some ran-dom be - liev - er!
19
JAMES: Oh, brother!
20
G2:
Mar - y nev - er had more kids!
22
G1:
Gos - pel writ - ers say she did!
24
God made Mar - y Jo - seph's wife.
26
G2:
She stayed pure all of her life!

Growing Up with the Son of God

Words by Linda Bonney Olin, 2013
Music by Benjamin Hanby, 1864; adapted by Linda Bonney Olin, 2013

(G1, G2, JAMES)

G1 & G2:

Must have no-ticed some-thing odd,

grow - ing up with the son of God!

G1:

Did - n't Je - sus give some clue?

G2:

Act - ing too good to be true?

JAMES: Not really...

G1:

Sure-ly such a spe-cial boy would-n't play with

104

14
G2:
com - mon toys. How did Je - sus
16
spend his day? Go off on his own to pray?
19
JAMES: Now that you mention it...
20
G1:
Did he shine in syn - a - gogue?
22
G2:
Did he heal the neigh - bor's dog?
24
G1:
Did he have a ho - ly look?
26
G2:
Mem - or - ize the ho - ly book?

Pro or Con

Words by Linda Bonney Olin, 2013
Music by Benjamin Hanby, 1864; adapted by Linda Bonney Olin, 2013

(G1, G2, JAMES)

G1 & G2:
First you claim you're fam-il-y, then speak like an en-e-my.

G1:
Are you call-ing Christ a fraud?

G2:
Do you call him Son of God?

JAMES: I was just getting to that...

G1:
"Spir-i-tual re-la-tion-ship" rolled so sweet-ly

G1 & G2:
from your lip. Are you try - ing

to de-ceive us a-bout what you be-lieve?

JAMES: I can explain!

G2:
Bet - ter make your mean - ing clear.

G1:
Nice and loud so we can hear!

G2:
Which side are you real - ly on?

G1 & G2:
Are you pro or are you con?

All That Counts

Words by Linda Bonney Olin, 2013
Music by Benjamin Hanby, 1864; adapted by Linda Bonney Olin, 2013

(ALL)

G2: James-'s sto-ry does ring true.

G1: I be - lieve him. INTERVIEWER: I do, too.

G1 & G2: Let's a - gree to dis - a - gree

on the fel - low's fam - ily tree.

JAMES: That's the spirit!

JAMES, G1 & G2: All that counts is hav-ing faith. JAMES: E-ven if you

JAMES, G1 & G2:

find it late. We be - lieve the

truth is this: Je-sus, our Re - deem-er, lives!

INTERVIEWER: Any closing remarks?

JAMES, G1 & G2:

We don't care what else you say,

please de - scribe us in this way:

ALL:

Serv - ants of the Liv - ing God

and of Je - sus Christ, our Lord!

Accompaniment for James's Ditties

Music by Benjamin Hanby, 1864; adapted by Linda Bonney Olin, 2013

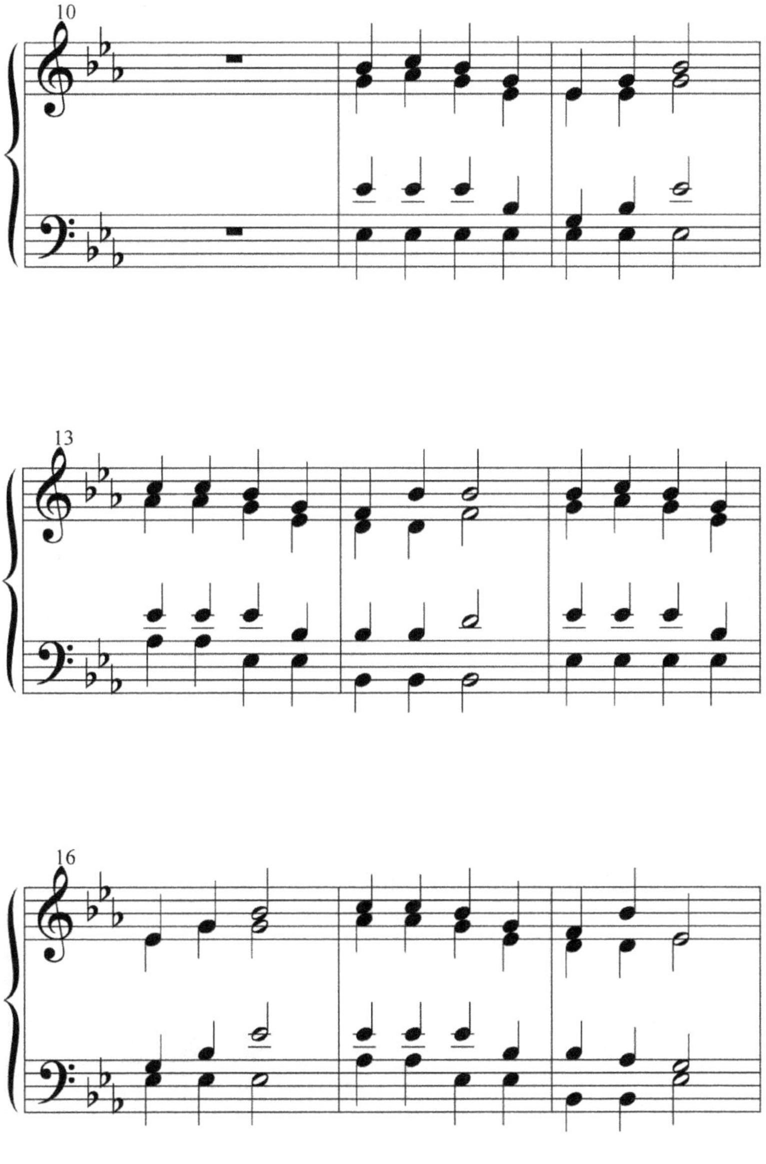
10
13
16

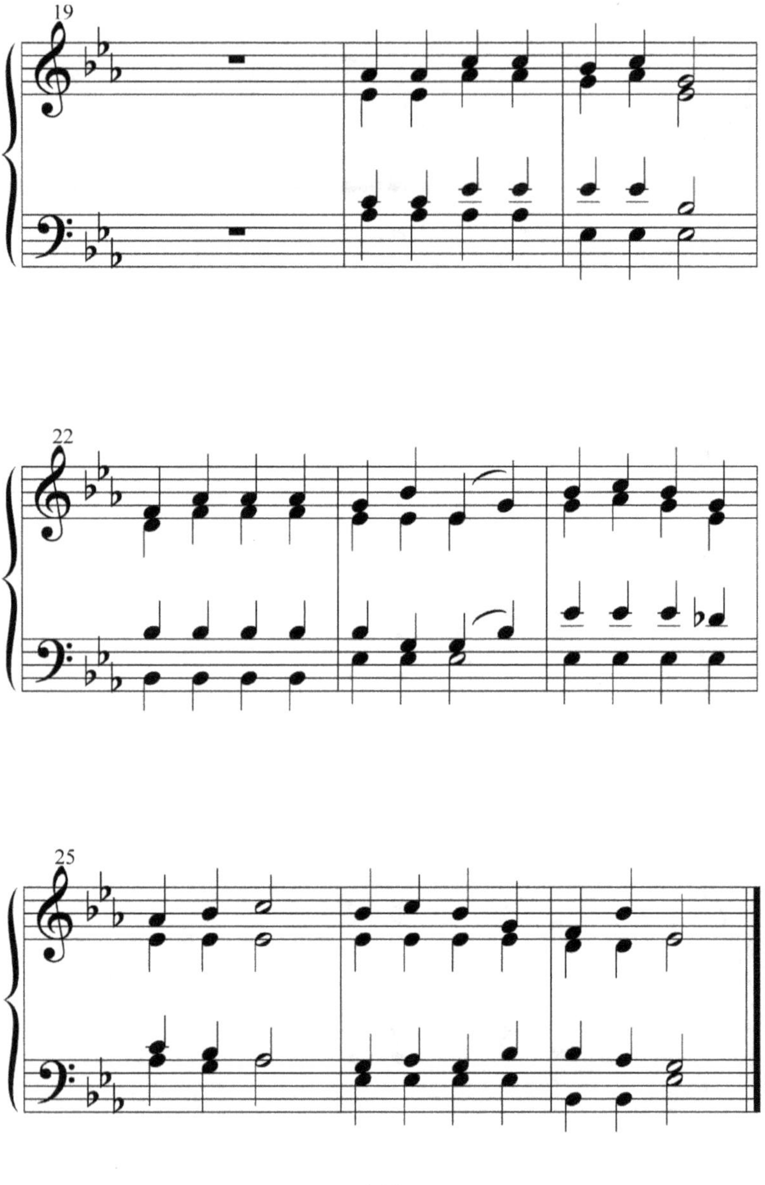
19
22
25

ABOUT THE AUTHOR

Linda Bonney Olin is a veteran leader of Bible studies and Sunday school programs for adults and children. She has been a lay speaker in the United Methodist Church since 1997. Her writing ministry has produced a wealth of dramas, songs, sermons, puppet plays, and special event programs for her own congregation and other churches. Her poems, devotions, short fiction, hymns, and Bible study materials have appeared in literary and devotional magazines, anthologies, and online publications.

Visit www.LindaBonneyOlin.com to contact Linda, learn about her and her work, and find a variety of resources for ministry, music, and more. Check the Audio page to hear samples of the music from this book and Linda's other songs and hymns.

ALSO BY LINDA BONNEY OLIN

The Sacrifice Support Group
A Dramatic Comedy for Lent

Laugh and learn along with a mixed bag of church characters challenged by their pastor to take a new look at the old tradition of giving something up for Lent. They resolve to offer personal sacrifices that glorify God and benefit their families and community—even the world!

Two twenty-minute acts. Cast: 1 M, 3 F; 3 M/F. Ideal for actors with limited mobility. Virtually no staging required. Easy to put on as Readers Theatre with little or no preparation.

Giving It Up for Lent
Bible Study, Drama, Discussion

Complete guide to leading a fun, life-changing, five-to-seven session study of Lenten sacrifice, featuring *The Sacrifice Support Group*. Includes an introductory look at Bible accounts of people who offered sacrifices to the Lord; in-depth discussion questions; and the drama script. For adults and older teens. Leader guide and optional workbook.

Now Sings My Soul
New Songs for the Lord

More than a hundred hymns and faith songs with lyrics by Linda Bonney Olin, presented in stanza format for easy reading and also in musical settings. Some feature original music; most are set to classic hymn tunes. Includes indexes of relevant scripture passages and suggested themes and occasions for use in devotions and worship.

Songs for the Lord
A Book of Twenty-Four Original Hymns and Faith Songs

A mix of congregational hymns, soulful solos, hand-clapping gospel, and humorous songs. Lyrics and melodies; no piano accompaniment. (Updated versions of some songs from this collection appear with full accompaniment in *Now Sings My Soul*.)

Were You There When They Crucified Our Lord?
Meditations on Calvary

Calvary through the eyes of those present when Jesus Christ was arrested and crucified, including:

- the Roman and religious authorities;
- the twelve;
- the women;
- the jeering onlookers.

Six chapters of scripture readings, meditations, songs, discussion questions, and prayers.

www.ingramcontent.com/pod-product-compliance
Lightning Source LLC
Chambersburg PA
CBHW060113050426

42448CB00010B/1857